Voices
In The Wilderness
School of the Prophets

Listen.Learn.Obey

Prophetic Manual

Adam LiVecchi | John Natale

Listen.Learn.Obey
Prophetic Manual

John Natale | Adam LiVecchi

Voices in the Wilderness | School of the Prophets

All scripture are taken from King James Version which is in Public Domain, unless otherwise noted.

Listen.Learn.Obey

ISBN 978-0-9835523-3-8

Printed in the United States of America

First Printed: November 2011

For more information on how to order this book go to
www.VoicesintheWilderness.us

Endorsements

There are many ministers in the body of Christ that call themselves prophets or prophetic people but haven't been trained in the word or in the sensitivity to hear God's voice. This manual will give those who hunger and thirst to develop an anointing and flow from the Holy Spirit that will mature them to use the prophetic gifts in the market place and in the church. This book is well needed in the body of Christ and I highly recommend it.

Prophet Jim Jorgensen
Sound the Trumpet Ministries International
www.soundthetrumpetministries.org

The Body of Christ especially in North America needs to go from being "non - Prophet" to "for – Prophet," and from pathetic to prophetic. Jesus declared to us that we, as His sheep, would hear His voice. Therefore, the act of hearing God's voice should be as normal as taking a deep breath or listening to the birds in the trees. I also really appreciate Adam and John focusing on subjects such as Biblical integrity, humility and purity, which are often found missing in other books on the prophetic. "Listen.Learn.Obey" is accessible, thorough and applicable to both new believers as well as mature Christians who want to go deeper in Christ. It is extremely timely and relevant!

Pastor Arthur Soto
Heaven's Gate Church
Passaic, New Jersey

I have known John for over almost two years. He was introduced to me at a time when I needed someone with his ear to listen to me and understand me, and to listen to the Holy Spirit to share with me what I needed to hear. His sensitivity to the Holy Spirit was a blessing beyond description. His gifting of discernment and encouragement has refreshed both my wife and me. You will be blessed by his ministry, his perception and his compassion. I heartily endorse John, the manual and his ministry. You are in for a blessing from the Lord through His servant, John!

Pastor Scott Fairchild
CrossRoad SouthBay Church
Gardena, California
www.crossroadsouthbay.com

John Natale is passionate for Jesus! He has a clear and sharp prophetic ministry that builds up the body of Christ. John has been a real blessing to me and my family and the members of our church. We are excited about this prophetic manual and look forward to using it in our church.

Pastor Daniel Donzelli
Little Flock Church
Schenectady, New York
www.littleflockchurch.com

If you hunger to walk in prophetic ministry Listen.Learn.Obey is for you. We have scores of books on prophetic ministry but this is a learners manual. This book puts practical tools in your hand. This book will not be an afternoon read but a seasonal soaking. You will work your way through this book and into a breakthrough. Adam LiVecchi is dedicated to God's own purpose of raising up a prophetic people.

Pastor Alan Hawkins
New Life City Church
Alberqurque, NM
www.NewLifeCity.org

☙

Adam and Sarah LiVecchi are personal friends of mine, I love them very much and I am honored to endorse Adam's newest book "Listen.Learn.Obey". In Matthew 16:18 Jesus said that the gates of hell would not prevail against the church. It's interesting to point out that gates are not mobile, they do not get up and attack, they are a fixed object. This is because the church is called to advance the Kingdom of Heaven and to live proactively instead of living reactively to the attacks of the enemy. Adam is a man of God who lives life proactively as he follows Jesus and this manual will equip and strengthen the body of Christ in the prophetic so that we can storm the gates of hell in all aspects of society. It's spiritual and practical, simple and yet profound. I highly endorse this manual especially for pastors and leaders who have a desire to be equipped and activated in the prophetic.

Nic Billman
Shores of Grace Ministries, a missionary and worship ministry rescuing women and children from prostitution in Brazil.
www.ShoresofGrace.com
www.ShoresMusic.com

Acknowledgments

We would like to thank Pastors David and Denise Greco for opening up King's Gate Church to us. A very special thank you to Julia Hali for editing. We would also like to thank Anthony Thompson for his graphic design work. John would like to thank his wife Nancy for all her help, and Adam would like to thank his wife Sarah for all her help as well.

Table of Contents

Operating in the Prophetic

Introduction

We would like to start by saying we are terribly sorry for how the prophetic ministry has been misrepresented, abused, misused and sold. Let us start by saying this Jesus is not for sale, the anointing is not for sale, a prophetic word should not be for sale, and dream interpretation should not be sold as a service. The fact that there is a market for prophetic words means Prophets and Prophetic teachers aren't finished with the work of equipping the saints just yet. We are not in this to slam anyone. Our desire is that Listen.Learn.Obey would be a piece to the puzzle to help equip the saints.

Introduction to the Prophetic

Study

(Adam LiVecchi)

Study | ˈstədē|
Noun (pl. studies)
1 - the devotion of time and attention to acquiring knowledge on an academic subject, esp. by means of books: the study of English | an application to continue full-time study.

We have defined study in the English language. Now it's time for a prophetic word because this is a prophetic manual. "Read and Study your Bible," thus saith the Lord. "*Study to show thyself approved unto God, a workman that needeth not to be ashamed, rightly dividing the word of truth.*" (2 Timothy 2:15)

In Greek, the word study also means to labor, be diligent, to be prompt or earnest, or also a forward endeavor. We have already learned one word in two languages, but we must be doers of the word not hearers only. In the verse above, Paul the Apostle is speaking to his spiritual son Timothy. These words echo through the centuries and are essential for all of us today. The scripture above is an apostolic command from one generation to the next. We might want to listen to a man who wrote more than half of the New Testament. We are commanded in scripture to study to show ourselves as approved unto God. Being an approved workman means we have no shame. It causes us to understand that we are called and chosen for the work of the ministry. The blood of Jesus makes us accepted in the beloved, but studying to show ourselves as an approved workman to God is what prepares us for the work. It's the word of God that prepares us for the work of God. As we rightly divided the word of truth, it rightly divides us.

"For the word of God is quick, and powerful, and sharper than any two-edged sword, piercing even to the dividing asunder of soul and spirit, and of the joints and marrow, and is a discerner of the thoughts and intents of the heart." (Hebrews 4:12)

The word is a divider and a discerner. It divides soul from spirit and discerns the thoughts and the intents of the heart. The thoughts would be what we think about and the intents would be why we think them. The word separates and makes clear that which needs to be understood and realized. When the word of God breaks in on a heart or mind, what was dark and obscure becomes illuminated and clear.

"Thy word is a lamp unto my feet, and a light unto my path". (Psalm 119:105)

The word deals with where we are and where we are going. The scripture is the lamp in which light breaks forth. The rhema or prophetic word comes from the Logos word. As prophetic people, we need to have a higher value for the scriptures. As much as we reverence Jesus will be as much as we honor his word. We honor his word by doing the work he has called us to.

Often when people read the Bible they often don't feel like they are actually getting or receiving something from God. The enemy relentlessly tries to use these kinds of feelings to bring discouragement. Discouragement often gives birth to unbelief and or deception, we must guard our heart from this sort of discouragement. When we read the scriptures and don't feel like we are getting something, it's then when the word is going deep into the roots of our heart. When we continue to eat the scroll and get the word on the inside of us we are actually preparing ourselves for future fruitfulness. Reading and studying is like making a deposit in our Spiritual bank account. Remember if you want to make a withdrawal you must first make a deposit. When was the last time you heard a message on studying the Bible? Sorry I had to ask that question. You will often hear messages on prayer and worship but not on studying. The question is why? One of the various answers could be because studying doesn't rouse up one's feelings as much as screaming and singing. Perhaps we need to study the scriptures and be silent as we wait on the voice of the Lord as much as we need to pray and worship. It's not one or the other; it's all of the above.

A lot of the problems that exist in the church are because people don't consistently ready, study and obey what the Bible says. A good deal of the prophetic movement is weak and flaky due to a lack of Biblical understanding. My desire is not to take shots at a target the size of Texas (the prophetic movement). The real goal of this section is to stir a hunger in your heart for God's word. If you get hungry, you will get fed; if you are full, you will naturally overflow. I believe the Lord is releasing a deep hunger in the earth now. Several years ago I had a vision in the spirit of my mind where there was a beautiful bride. She opened her mouth as if to smile or speak; when she did, it was as if this grown woman was teething like a child. In that moment I sensed the whisper of God from the person of the Holy Spirit saying, "Feed the church— she's getting hungry." The teething meant that teeth were coming in soon and there would be a season of discomfort until they grow in. I now believe that God is releasing a hunger that will cause the church to get fed. To say it simply, it's not your Pastor's job to feed you; it's your job to position yourself in such a way that you are receiving from God yourself. Studying the scriptures for yourself is necessary, whether it's popular or not. Personally, I think if we understood God's primary intention when he gave us the scriptures we would approach studying a bit differently. In Matthew 10:16, Jesus commanded his disciples to, *"be ye therefore wise."* Paul the apostle tells us one of the ways we become wise.

"And that from a child thou hast known the holy scriptures, which are able to make thee wise unto salvation through faith which is in Christ Jesus. All scripture is given by inspiration of God, and is profitable for doctrine, for reproof, for correction, for instruction in righteousness: That the man of God may be perfect, thoroughly furnished unto all good works." (2 Timothy 3:15-17)

The Holy Scriptures are able to make us wise unto salvation. The word of God is inspired and infallible. It is applicable to every area of life. We are furnished by the word for good works. When God speaks, he actually intends us to act on what he says. We will get into this more later.

We don't interpret the Bible; the Bible interprets the Bible. The word of God is infallible because the author cannot lie for he is the truth. If studying the word is boring or tedious, something is definitely wrong. I will quote from my little brother, Aaron LiVecchi's recent Twitter post. "Study doesn't feel tedious when you are in love with the author." When we love God, we begin to have a deep affection for his word. Out of the abundance of the heart the mouth speaks. How we feel about the word is how we feel about the very heart of God. When the true prophetic word is rejected, it's actually Jesus who is being rejected. Our response to the word is critical. Studying the word with sincerity of heart prepares our heart to respond properly to the prophetic word. The word keeps us from error.

"Jesus answered and said unto them, Ye do err, not knowing the scriptures, nor the power of God." (Matthew 22:29)

To really walk in truth we need the scriptures and the power of God, not one or the other but both.

What is the Bible really about? Good question. It's about Jesus and his plan of redemption. That seems simple but we often get distracted on bunny trails of lesser things. When our path is not straight, it's actually because something is not right in our heart. The solution is the word of God.

"Thy word have I hid in mine heart, that I might not sin against thee." (Psalm 119:11)

All sin is directly against God because Jesus tasted death for every man. So God gave Jesus to pay for us, and our sins are directly against him because he paid for them in full. When the word is really hidden in our heart, we are kept from sin and we live godly in Christ Jesus. Living godly means being holy and fruitful. It means God's word is in us and his power moves through us by his Holy Spirit. It means when we speak, Jesus says amen to our message and signs and wonders follow us and point to him. If you are following Jesus, signs and wonders will follow you. Don't follow signs and wonders, be one. To get right down to my main point, the scriptures are primarily about Jesus, and the Father and the Holy Spirit are so excited about Jesus! The Father says, "This is my well beloved Son, hear him." The Holy Spirit says, "Yeah I get to remind you of all that Jesus said. Wow, I love my job." I am paraphrasing what I know to be in the heart of God. To hear, we must listen and to be reminded we must be willing to remember. If the primary purpose of the scriptures are to reveal Jesus and we want to know him, perhaps we should be serious about studying. More than we want to know God, God desires to be known. God doesn't operate in the realm of need; he operates in the realm of desire, and he doesn't need to be known; he desires us to know him. The primary way God desires to reveal himself is by the Holy Spirit through the scriptures. Even real prophets who have open visions and encouters with angels of the Lord don't have them as often as they read and study the word.

But I will show thee that which is noted in the scripture of truth: and there is none that holdeth with me in these things, but Michael your prince. (Daniel 10:21)

Here Jesus appears to Daniel to reveal to Daniel something written in the Scriptures that was pertinent to him in that time. What is interesting is that Jesus showed up to discuss prophetic scriptures with Daniel. Could you imagine what it would be like for a glorified Jesus to appear to you and give you a quick Bible study? That would be amazing. What is also amazing is we see Jesus doing something similar at a later time with a few of his disciples. Keep in mind the He in the next verse is Jesus.

"And they said one to another, Did not our heart burn within us, while he talked with us by the way, and while he opened to us the scriptures?" (Luke 24:32)

The word of God is not just meant to be read or studied it is also meant to be revealed and experienced because it is alive. In the Old Testament, Jeremiah had a similar encounter with the same Jesus.

"Then I said, I will not make mention of him, nor speak any more in his name. But his word was in mine heart as a burning fire shut up in my bones, and I was weary with forbearing, and I could not stay." (Jeremiah 20:9)

Here is the New Jersey translation of Jeremiah's experience, "he was filled up with God's word so he would be shut up despite what the cost was." God doesn't change and neither does the power of his word. I firmly believe God desires the fire of his word to burn on the altar of our hearts so that we can't help put preach Jesus to those who need him but don't have him.

It's like we are going back in time to see what God has for us now. After Jesus' resurrection he walked with two of his disciples for about 7.5 miles. Here is what they talked about. *"And beginning at Moses and all the prophets, he expounded unto them in all the scriptures the things concerning himself."* (Luke 24:27)

The resurrected Jesus is revealing himself to them in the context of the written word of God. This is necessary today; when God reveals himself to us in the context of the written word, it brings great maturity and stability to our lives that goes beyond "emotionalism". You can see how much revelation someone has of Jesus based on the decision he or she makes. When we mature in our faith the only thing that moves us is Jesus. This is the place God is taking the church before the Lord Jesus returns and touches his feet down on Mt Zion. Jesus later appeared to the rest of his disciples opening the scriptures to them. About forty days later, the never-ending revival started in the upper room on the day of Pentecost. Before Jesus poured out his Holy Spirit, he opened the scriptures to them. This happened so when God showed up they had language for it. Peter preached the message he did on the day of Pentecost for two reasons: 1. Jesus opened the scriptures to him. 2. The Holy Spirit came upon him.

Genesis or in the beginning God was creating through his Word, or his Son Jesus. Then Moses receives the Law. The Law is really about Jesus who will come to fulfill it. Jesus is every feast; he is every sacrifice; he is the once and for all sacrifice. The Psalms are songs worshiping him. The Proverbs are his wisdom; he is wisdom. The Prophets prophesied his coming. In the Gospels he came and did what he said. Acts is what happens when people do what he said. The Epistles are the intricate formation of different people coming into One person—Christ. The Revelation is the revelation of Jesus Christ not the anti-Christ. People who live in fear see the book of Revelation as the revelation of the anti-christ. People who are in love see the book of revelation as the heart of God fully unveiled in the person of Jesus Christ. As you study the scriptures Jesus will open them to you.

Questions

1. Are you going to commit to study?

_____

_____

_____

_____

2. Where and when will you begin? Why are you studying?

_____

_____

_____

_____

3. Do you think there would be a benefit to studying in a group setting? If so why? Then do it as the Holy Spirit leads with whom the Holy Spirit leads.

_____

_____

_____

_____

Prayer of Impartation

Father I ask you to release a supernatural hunger to me for your Word. I want to eat the scroll so the Word becomes flesh in my life. Help me to be diligent in being a doer of the word. Open the scriptures to me and let Christ Jesus be unveiled to me like never before. Let your word burn like a fire in my heart until it consistently comes out of my mouth. Let my words be full of grace and truth. Help me to properly represent you. I ask you all these things believing that you will do them in Jesus' name.

Scriptures to Meditate On

• John 5:39 *"Search the scriptures; for in them ye think ye have eternal life: and they are they which testify of me."*
• Jeremiah 23:29 *"Is not my word like as a fire? saith the LORD; and like a hammer that breaketh the rock in pieces?"*
• Luke 24:44-45 *"And he said unto them, These are the words which I spoke unto you, while I was yet with you, that all things must be fulfilled, which were written in the law of Moses, and in the prophets, and in the psalms, concerning me. Then opened he their understanding, that they might understand the scriptures,"*

Exercise

I challenge you to speak in tongues for 30 minutes before you do your next Bible study. This just may revive your study time. If you speak mysteries to God, he will speak mysteries to you. If you do not speak in tongues ask the Holy Spirit to fill you and give you the gift of tongues, that you might speak mysteries to God and edify yourself.

The Posture of a Learner

(Adam LiVecchi)

Posture |ˈpäsCHər|
Noun
1 a position of a person's body when standing or sitting: she stood in a flamboyant posture with her hands on her hips | good posture will protect your spine.
2 a particular way of dealing with or considering something; an approach or attitude: labor unions adopted a more militant posture in wage negotiations.

The word *learn* is found 32 times in the Bible. Matthew 11:28-30 says, "*Come unto me, all ye that labor and are heavy laden, and I will give you rest. Take my yoke upon you, and learn of me; for I am meek and lowly in heart: and ye shall find rest unto your souls. For my yoke is easy, and my burden is light.*" The way we learn is by continually coming to him. The posture of a learner is one of humility. The truth is that Jesus is and has what we need and we need to come to him to receive only what he can give. The humility and the meekness of Jesus are what draw those who are in need of him. We need to learn because we don't know everything, just recognizing our need for Jesus really pleases the Father. However, recognizing a need is not enough; we need to come to him so that need is met by him. Humility and honor create a great atmosphere for learning. Humility recognizes its need to learn and honoring the teacher is key to receiving all the teacher has to offer you. Putting into practice is what solidifies what you have learned. Learners haven't learned until they have done what they are learning. In doing we are still continually learning. Teachers who aren't learning anymore shouldn't be teaching. Learning is actually what qualifies you to teach.

During the learning process people will make mistakes. After the learning, people will make mistakes. Pencils have erasers because people make mistakes.

Whiteout was created because people using pens make mistakes. Stain stick was created because people make mistakes. Auto body shops exist and thrive off people who make mistakes. Jails in America are filled because people make mistakes. Computer keyboards have a backspace or delete button because people make mistakes. Jesus died because people make mistakes. The key to living a life that is naturally productive, spiritually fruitful and just plain interesting is learning. Those who do what they have learned usually succeed if they continue to persevere. Learning requires perseverance because there will be times where learning is not any fun. The sacrifice of learning leads to the responsibility of teaching and the privilege of being a teacher. We live in a time in human history where learning is easier and faster than ever because of technology. If you learn better by hearing you can buy an audio book. If you are a visual learner, there are visuals for you to learn what you need to, while others just read to learn. You can put a word or question into the Google search bar and in seconds you will have results. Unfortunately always learning something doesn't mean one actually knows it. In second Timothy Paul speaks about perilous times. (Just in case you haven't seen the news lately, those are the times we live in.) Then he makes a comment about learning.

"Ever learning, and never able to come to the knowledge of the truth." (2 Timothy 3:7)

It is very possible to know about the truth but to not know the Truth. The truth that is experienced makes you free. When people only know about the truth they are not yet free until they personally know the truth. It's experience that solidifies learning. Here is brief example. You are driving 78 mph hour in a 55 mph speed zone and a cop pulls you over. You are going to get a big ticket. You can tell the officer you know the speed limit but he is going to tell you, "Great now meet the speeding ticket." We truly know what we live. All leadership in the Kingdom is by example. I tell this to Pastors every once in a while. "Your people will do what you do, not what you say." If you tell them soul winning is important and don't show up to do outreaches with them, your actions are actually undermining your teaching. Jesus calls that hypocrisy. Often people lack spiritual authority because their life style and the actions are not in agreement.

You are reading this manual because you want to learn, which is good news. There are many things we need to learn and we all learn differently. We will touch on a few things we need to learn in the Kingdom, especially when it comes to the prophetic. Coming to Jesus is how we get to know him, which is the most important thing in life, which is why it is commandment number one. Commandment number one needs to be priority number one as well or we will be out of order. Anything that is out of order is dysfunctional. Any other desire that comes before knowing God is idolatry. Ministry, church, missions trips can all be idolatry if they take a higher priority than knowing Jesus. Granted as you do that stuff you get to know him. However, setting apart time to focus on Jesus is the fuel for all those other things. All authentic ministry proceeds from the secret place. The stewardship we have received causes us to be stewards of mysteries; mysteries are released and unveiled in the secret place. Learning to say no to other things and yes to Jesus is of the utmost importance. Those who can't say yes to Jesus will never be able to say no to self. When Jesus said to come to me, he really meant it. He didn't say come to church, or come to a prayer meeting; he said come to me. Church and prayer meetings are great, however you need a personal relationship with Jesus which comes through spending time alone with Him. Church and prayer meetings should be times when we "boldly approach the throne of grace." If individuals respond to Jesus, the corporate church will respond. If individuals don't respond, the corporate church will not be able to respond properly to the invitation Jesus sent out. This is a personal invitation for us to get to know him intimately. Out of all things I do, my absolute favorite thing to do is spend time alone with Jesus. I can honestly say he is my very best friend. Without him I would be in jail or dead and burning in hell. There is no one I spend as much time with. When I come to him, I am not seeking him because he found me when I was not even looking for him. However, I am focusing on him and we are communicating, which is relationship not hide and go seek.

Let's see the ultimate posture of a learner. Luke 10:38-42 says, "*Now it came to pass, as they went, that he entered into a certain village: and a certain woman named Martha received him into her house. And she had a sister called Mary, which also sat at Jesus' feet, and heard his word. But Martha was cumbered about much serving, and came to him, and said, Lord, dost thou not care that my sister hath left me to serve alone? bid her therefore that she help me. And Jesus answered and said unto her, Martha, Martha, thou art careful and troubled about many things: But one thing is needful: and Mary hath chosen that good part, which shall not be taken away from her.*"

Mary is the only one who sat at the feet of Jesus to hear his word. This has a cultural implication that we need to understand. She was not only listening to his message but she was humbling herself and making herself subservient or subject to his authority. She positioned herself in such a way that the word would not be taken from her. This same Mary anointed Jesus for burial; she prophetically could see the cross ahead because she positioned herself as a learner. Even before we are servers we are learners. Her posture can be explained in two words humility and proximity. Her posture demonstrated humility because she was at a low and humble place, near his feet. Her posture demonstrated proximity because she was so close to Jesus no one could get in between her and him. The word needful in the verse above actually means occupation. Mary's job was actually to position herself as a learner and hear the voice of Jesus. I want to propose to you that the most important thing in life is that you and I would position ourselves to hear God's voice. To further drive home my point of the cultural implication of sitting at someone's feet let's look to the book of Acts.

"I am verily a man which am a Jew, born in Tarsus, a city in Cilicia, yet brought up in this city at the feet of Gamaliel, and taught according to the perfect manner of the law of the fathers, and was zealous toward God, as ye all are this day." (Acts 22:3)

This is Paul the Apostle speaking of his life prior to his life changing encounter with Jesus on the road to Damascus. Sitting at someone's feet is the posture of learning, it's part of the discipleship process. Jesus is still looking for those who would live their whole entire lives with this very same posture. Biblical discipleship means we become fully subject to Jesus and his word.

Often the learning process is painful and tedious, but it is truly priceless. The lessons we truly learn will later lead to fruitfulness in our lives and ministries. The learning process is like the dying of a seed. Jesus was fully God and fully man. Even he learned obedience through the things he suffered. It is death that gives birth to resurrection life.

"Though he were a Son, yet learned he obedience by the things which he suffered."
(Hebrews 5:8)

The greatest way to learn is by obedience. Jesus had choices to make; he always made the right ones. His right decisions caused him to suffer for righteousness' sake. Through his obedience he learned suffering by experience. Learners eventually mature. God is maturing the church in this hour and it is a beautiful thing. Even now many people are experiencing growing pains. If Jesus who was God in the flesh submitted to the learning process, we need to build a bridge and get over ourselves and fully submit to the learning process. We do have the most amazing teacher ever in the Holy Spirit. The Holy Spirit is very committed to our learning. If we position ourselves properly in the learning process, we will be mature believers whose lives paint a picture to the world that looks and smells like Christ Jesus. God is so serious about us learning he put a teacher on the inside of us. God's grace has positioned us to be successful because of the indwelling presence of his Holy Spirit for those who believe. We as believers in Jesus have a default posture already set for us; we just need to stay the course. The more you get to know Jesus it's like the good news gets better. When we posture ourselves correctly today, we will be where we need to be tomorrow. If we are faithful with tomorrow, we will leave an inheritance to the next generation, and truly our ceiling can be their floor. In the Kingdom the only direction is forward. The only possibility in the Kingdom is increase; therefore, if we live a life in full subjection to the King and his commands, the next generation will truly begin where we left off. In the Kingdom this is the only option.

Questions

1. Have you positioned yourself as a learner?

_____

_____

_____

_____

2. Is there a specific person God desires you to learn from if so who is it?

_____

_____

_____

_____

3. Are you willing to be accountable to the person God wants you to learn from?

_____

_____

_____

_____

Prayer of Impartation

Father thank you for giving me the greatest teacher ever, thank you that he will teach me all things and lead me into all truth. Bring me into healthy relationships in the body of Christ so that I may learn all that you desire me to know in your timing. Teach me your ways as I listen to and walk with you.

Scriptures to Meditate On

• Deuteronomy 4:10 *"Specially the day that thou stoodest before the LORD thy God in Horeb, when the LORD said unto me, Gather me the people together, and I will make them hear my words, that they may learn to fear me all the days that they shall live upon the earth, and that they may teach their children."*
• Isaiah 1:17-19 *"Learn to do well; seek judgment, relieve the oppressed, judge the fatherless, plead for the widow. Come now, and let us reason together, saith the LORD: though your sins be as scarlet, they shall be as white as snow; though they be red like crimson, they shall be as wool. If ye be willing and obedient, ye shall eat the good of the land:"*
• John 14:26 *"But the Comforter, which is the Holy Ghost, whom the Father will send in my name, he shall teach you all things, and bring all things to your remembrance, whatsoever I have said unto you."*
• Titus 3:14 *"And let ours also learn to maintain good works for necessary uses, that they be not unfruitful."*

Exercise

The next time you go to a church service or watch one, try taking some notes. Capture the main themes from the person who is teaching. Then discuss how you can apply what you have heard. This seems practical but it is actually spiritual. When you value what you have received, God will give you more. Good students make great teachers. So be teachable and willing to act on what you have learned.

Learning to Listen

(Adam LiVecchi)

listen |ˈlisən|
verb [no obj.]
give one's attention to a sound: evidently he was not listening | sit and listen to the radio.
• take notice of and act on what someone says; respond to advice or a request: I told her over and over again, but she wouldn't listen.
• make an effort to hear something; be alert and ready to hear something: they listened for sounds from the baby's room.

"Wherefore, my beloved brethren, let every man be swift to hear, slow to speak, slow to wrath: For the wrath of man worketh not the righteousness of God. Wherefore lay apart all filthiness and superfluity of naughtiness, and receive with meekness the engrafted word, which is able to save your souls. But be ye doers of the word, and not hearers only, deceiving your own selves." (James 1:19-22)

Here James is not asking us to be slow to speak; he is commanding us. He commands us to be quick to hear and slow to speak because often we are not. The key to listening is actually being quiet. Often people who are quick to speak are also quick to get angry. Their anger is not usually a righteous anger; it's actually a lack of self-control. When self-control is not present, it is usually because there is a deep inward brokenness in a person, and they are literally not able to contain or control themselves because of the brokenness. We are supposed to overflow Holy Spirit, not leak from the brokenness of our soul realm. Someone who is always talking about others is someone who is leaking from the soul realm. Someone who is always speaking about and demonstrating Jesus is overflowing with Holy Spirit. If we want to receive the engrafted word that brings healing and salvation, sometimes we just need to sit down and be quiet. One thing that I learned early in my relationship with God is that it is better to listen to him than to tell him what he already knows. I am not de-valuing our supplications; I am saying that we don't live by our supplications but by every word that proceeds from his mouth.

"Incline your ear, and come unto me: hear, and your soul shall live; and I will make an everlasting covenant with you, even the sure mercies of David. Behold, I have given him for a witness to the people, a leader and commander to the people." (Isaiah 55:3)

The health of our soul is found in our ability to come to Jesus and listen to him. Proverbs 4:20-23 says, *"My son, attend to my words; incline thine ear unto my sayings. Let them not depart from thine eyes; keep them in the midst of thine heart. For they are life unto those that find them, and health to all their flesh. Keep thy heart with all diligence; for out of it are the issues of life."* Listening begins with our ears but it also has to do with our eyes, heart and mind. The way we diligently guard our heart is by continually inclining our ear. Diligence is made manifest on the outside by perseverance on the inside. We are strengthened to persevere by the word that is proceeding from the mouth of God.

The key to learning is listening and the key to listening is silence. Listening is something that is a learned behavior. It is not natural for someone to be a good listener; especially in a culture (Western Secular) that says your opinion and feelings is the truth. Listening is a developed skill. Usually good listeners are patient people, with a little more understanding than the average person. People who are not good listeners often have lots of broken relationships. The strength of our ability to communicate is seen in our ability to listen. Most people are actually thinking of their response instead of listening to the person they are communicating with. That is not actually talking with someone; it's more like talking at them. Talking to someone requires listening. We have the Bible because over the course of a few thousands years lots of people were listening to God and wrote down what he said. The heroes of faith in Hebrews 11 are the ones who acted on what they heard. The key to living a powerful life of faith is found in listening to God for faith comes by hearing the words of God. Our ability to speak is rooted in our ability to listen. Listening requires discipline and self-control. Discipline is for the ability to pay attention and self-control helps us not to interrupt the person we are communicating with. I have been guilty of doing both of these things in the same conversation. God has been dealing with me about this stuff for sometime now. About a year ago, I wouldn't have been able to write this without feeling like a total hypocrite. I am sharing my failures with you that you might succeed in being a good listener. For the married people, one of the keys to a good healthy marriage is listening. For those of you who are not married yet, learn how to listen now because it will save you problems later. Any deficiencies in our relationships with Jesus usually manifest in our relationships with people—ask me how I know. Many times un-confessed sin leads to damaged or broken relationships. Those who are not good listeners are often confused, and those who are not listened to are often deeply frustrated and can wind up bitter if they don't guard their hearts. An unguarded heart will lead to deaf ears. Ears that are not open, means a mind will not be renewed. An un-renewed mind cannot prove or discern the will of God. Often prophetic people can tell everyone what is the will of God for their lives but don't know the will of God for their own life. This is dysfunctional and out of order and God is maturing people out of this kind of futile and immature behavior. Often this behavior is manifested when people's priorities are out of order. We must value our relationship with Jesus and his will for our lives more than a prophetic word. Prophetic words should be birthed from relationship, not from a need to perform or entertain church or conference junkies.

A consistent life of prayer is one of the keys to growing in relationship with Jesus and effectiveness in ministry.

"Let us therefore come boldly unto the throne of grace, that we may obtain mercy, and find grace to help in time of need." (Hebrews 4:16)

I want to propose to you that we receive grace when God opens up his mouth and speaks. Jesus came full of grace and truth. His words are truth and they were seasoned in grace.

"Let no corrupt communication proceed out of your mouth, but that which is good to the use of edifying, that it may minister grace unto the hearers." (Ephesians 4:29)

Our words are supposed to minister grace to the hearers because Jesus' did. We can't give what we don't have and we receive by listening. Often in prayer people make supplications or requests of or to God, but don't wait long enough for him to speak back to them. Listening requires our attention; we give our attention to those we have affection for.

"Hear, O Israel: The LORD our God is one LORD: And thou shalt love the LORD thy God with all thine heart, and with all thy soul, and with all thy might. And these words, which I command thee this day, shall be in thine heart." (Deuteronomy 6:4-6)

Here God is requiring his people to listen to him. Before he commands them to love him, he requires them to listen and draw near to him. It's in listening to God that we are empowered to love him. This is consistent in the New Testament as well.

"If ye love me, keep my commandments." (John 14:15)

Our love for God is manifested in our obedience to his commands. This revelation was released as Jesus was speaking to his disciples. It's in listening to God that we are able to keep his commands. Silence is necessary. God one day will demand silence from the whole world.

"Be silent, O all flesh, before the LORD: for he is raised up out of his holy habitation." (Zechariah 2:13)

Silence is the stillness of the soul, and Stillness is the silence of the body. Both silence and stillness are missing from our busy lives. A modern term for this practice is soaking. Others call it waiting on the Lord; either way God's voice and his presence are what we are taking in and receiving through Jesus Christ. There is only one way to God and that is through his Son Jesus Christ. Here are two verses with keys in them to help us learn how to wait on the Lord.

"Rest in the LORD, and wait patiently for him: fret not thyself because of him who prospereth." (Psalm 37:7)

"The LORD is good unto them that wait for him, to the soul that seeketh him. It is good that a man should both hope and quietly wait for the salvation of the LORD." (Lamentations 3:25-26)

In these two verses there are three words we need to apply in our times of waiting on the Lord. We need to begin with hope or expectancy. Meaning we need to come to God believing that he is a rewarder of those who diligently seek him. As we wait, we need to do it quietly and patiently. The word quietly in Hebrew actually means still and silent. This is what the Bible says; it's not my opinion. We wait on God because we want to hear his voice, we want to know him, and we need direction and purpose for our lives. Those are just some of the many reasons why we wait on the Lord. God renews the strength of those who wait on him. Let me say it point blank— those who don't wait on God are weak and will burn themselves out in no time. As a matter of fact it probably won't even take a decade to burn yourself out if you don't wait on God. The will of God will burn you up not burn you out. God wants to be loved, and he wants to be known. He is absolutely crazy about you. Jesus has the most amazing personality and he invites us to love him with all that we are. That is our greatest ministry invitation ever.

"And thou shalt love the Lord thy God with all thy heart, and with all thy soul, and with all thy mind, and with all thy strength: this is the first commandment." (Mark 12:30)

We love God with our heart by setting our affections on things above. We love him with our soul by surrendering our will for his. We love him with our mind by thinking on Jesus and those things he has commanded us to think on in his word.

"Finally, brethren, whatsoever things are true, whatsoever things are honest, whatsoever things are just, whatsoever things are pure, whatsoever things are lovely, whatsoever things are of good report; if there be any virtue, and if there be any praise, think on these things." (Philippians 4:8)

We love him with our strength by serving, fasting and becoming weak, and finally by being still. It will require all of our strength to spend time being still before the Lord. It will take all of our strength and a half-pound of grace to be still and silent and wait patiently until we receive what we are asking and hoping for.

"Be still, and know that I am God: I will be exalted among the heathen, I will be exalted in the earth." (Psalm 46:10)

In stillness the knowledge of God is released; when the knowledge of God is released, it carries with it the knowledge of his will.

Several years ago I went through a painful time in my life. A Pastor who I deeply respected rejected me because I was a knucklehead. Anyway I tried to humble myself and apologize. I also tried to work things out with him, but it didn't seem to really clear things up fully. It was painful for my family and I. Part of it was my fault, and part of it was not and the devil may have had his hand in on this one as well. During that time in my life I did plumbing work on the side. I had just came home from work. When I walked upstairs to my room, God was there, and I fell to the floor immediately. I called my family to come up stairs. I yelled, "God is in my room, come quick!" My father, mother, brother and I laid silently in the manifest presence of the Lord for about one hour." Four people from New Jersey without one college degree lying silently in God's presence for an hour was a verifiable miracle that had just been documented. The cloud of God's glory that rested in Solomon's temple came to my house in Little Ferry, NJ that afternoon. God's presence was visible and tangible, even a straight up heathen could have seen it. The presence of the Lord washed over us, cleansed us and brought healing. It was a day I will never forget. As I laid there on the floor in silence God said to me, "Adam I am not rejecting you; I approve of you and my manifest presence is the proof, don't seek the approval of men." All that pain in my heart provoked a visit by the Almighty. As I am writing this I have wept thinking about the faithfulness of God. Just stop and Selah for a moment. Think of his faithfulness in your life and thank him for all he has done before you continue reading. When the manifest presence of the Lord shows up, the most natural thing to do is be quiet. When God shows up, it's because he wants to speak to you. He actually thinks he has the right to speak to you. He expects that you will listen so just quiet your soul and open your heart and you will be able to hear God. The biggest distraction from hearing God is self, or in other words an un-surrendered will. To receive God's will we must surrender ours. His will is our surrender.

Questions

1. Do you struggle to be still or silent? If so, why?

_____

_____

_____

_____

2. How can you know what you are hearing is from God or not?

_____

_____

_____

_____

3. Will you make time to be still and silent and wait on the voice of God?

_____

_____

_____

_____

Prayer of Impartation

Father, I thank you for your peace, cause me to be silent and still your presence. Help me to come to you with a greater expectancy than ever before. God give me the grace and the patience to wait in your presence until I receive what you have and hear what you are saying.

Scripture to Meditate On

• Job 37:14 *"Hearken unto this, O Job: stand still, and consider the wondrous works of God."*
• Psalm 4:4 *"Stand in awe, and sin not: commune with your own heart upon your bed, and be still. Selah."*
• Psalm 84:4 *"Blessed are they that dwell in thy house: they will be still praising thee. Selah."*

Exercise

Now is your chance to be a doer of the word. Get your Bible, a notebook or writing device, laptop, i-Pad or something that wants to be an i-Pad. Sit down and quietly read for 15 minutes. Then close your Bible invite the Holy Spirit to speak to you, ask him to reveal Jesus. Pray what is on your heart and then be still and silent for 15 minutes. Write down the thoughts that come to your mind, or write down any visions you may have. Write down anything God says to you. Please understand this is not a discipline; it's a privilege. (You may enjoy Jesus so much that perhaps you will make a habit out of this privilege of being with him and listening to his voice.)

Growing to Understand

(Adam LiVecchi)

understand | ˌəndərˈstand|
verb (past and past participle understood)
1 [with obj.] perceive the intended meaning of (words, a language, or speaker): he didn't understand a word I said | he could usually make himself understood | [with clause] : she understood what he was saying.
• perceive the significance, explanation, or cause of (something): she didn't really understand the situation | [with clause] : he couldn't understand why we burst out laughing | [no obj.] : you don't understand—she has left me.
• be sympathetically or knowledgeably aware of the character or nature of: Picasso understood color | [with clause] : I understand how you feel.
• interpret or view (something) in a particular way: as the term is usually understood, legislation refers to regulations and directives.
2 [with clause] infer something from information received (often used as a polite formula in conversation): I understand you're at art school | [with obj.] : as I understood it, she was flying back to New Zealand tomorrow.

"And they said, Go to, let us build us a city and a tower, whose top may reach unto heaven; and let us make us a name, lest we be scattered abroad upon the face of the whole earth. And the LORD came down to see the city and the tower, which the children of men builded. And the LORD said, Behold, the people is one, and they have all one language; and this they begin to do: and now nothing will be restrained from them, which they have imagined to do. Go to, let us go down, and there confound their language, that they may not understand one another's speech. So the LORD scattered them abroad from thence upon the face of all the earth: and they left off to build the city. Therefore is the name of it called Babel; because the LORD did there confound the language of all the earth: and from thence did the LORD scatter them abroad upon the face of all the earth." (Genesis 11:4-9)

In the beginning of this passage we learn that God is not distant from the affairs of men. Biblically speaking Deists are absolutely wrong. We immediately learn that God is listening to human conversation. This reveals his omniscience and omnipresence. We come to understand from Genesis 1:26 and Genesis 11:7 that God is plural, meaning one God in three persons. The Triune God, Father Son and Holy Spirit is a very important foundational understanding that is necessary to further understand God's plan of redemption and how God operates prophetically. God is Prophetic. So these people unite to make a tower to the heavens. Perhaps they were trying to make their own way to heaven or God, and he cut that off swiftly because there is only one way and that is through Jesus. God knew their building would reach their goal of the heavens, so he went down and confounded their language. God's judgment or verdict against their soulish unity was confusion. They went from being able to communicate and understand and accomplish what was virtually impossible to being scattered abroad and unable to communicate. This is the first place the Bible uses the word understand. Before God confounded or confused their language, they were able to communicate and understand one another. The possibility of their success was built on their agreement of purpose and their ability to communicate with each other and understand one another. So the curse of confusion was released and their plans were foiled. Then God scattered them upon the face of all the earth. During that time all of the earth became occupied with people. It is not clear how this happened. It may have been supernatural and it may have been migration. Scripture doesn't really say, so we are not going to make it say something it doesn't say. God scattering the people abroad is setting the stages for Noah and the flood and eventually his promise to Abraham. The whole point of the promise of God to Abraham was so that Jesus could go forth.

> "But now in Christ Jesus ye who sometimes were far off are made nigh by the blood of Christ. For he is our peace, who hath made both one, and hath broken down the middle wall of partition between us; Having abolished in his flesh the enmity, even the law of commandments contained in ordinances; for to make in himself of twain one new man, so making peace; And that he might reconcile both unto God in one body by the cross, having slain the enmity thereby: And came and preached peace to you which were afar off, and to them that were nigh. For through him we both have access by one Spirit unto the Father."
> (Ephesians 2:13-18)

So the blood of Jesus washed us and brought us near. The wall of partition has been broken between Jew and Gentile, and the cross slays cultural enmity that existed. The cross of Jesus has also paid for prejudice to be broken as well. The veil was torn when Jesus was crucified; the separation between God and his presence has been fully abolished in Jesus Christ. He came so that we would live in him and he would live in us. He came to restore us back to fellowship with God and communication with him and one another. The cross has paid for the curse of babel, which is confusion to be broken. The cross has made a way to God through the veil of Jesus' flesh. In Acts chapter 2 heaven came down. Instead of man trying to make his way to God, God the Holy Spirit came to dwell in men. Instead of receiving the judgment of confusion that the people of Babel experienced, the Apostles received the promise of the Father.

"And when the day of Pentecost was fully come, they were all with one accord in one place. And suddenly there came a sound from heaven as of a rushing mighty wind, and it filled all the house where they were sitting. And there appeared unto them cloven tongues like as of fire, and it sat upon each of them. And they were all filled with the Holy Ghost, and began to speak with other tongues, as the Spirit gave them utterance. And there were dwelling at Jerusalem Jews, devout men, out of every nation under heaven. Now when this was noised abroad, the multitude came together, and were confounded, because that every man heard them speak in his own language. And they were all amazed and marveled, saying one to another, Behold, are not all these which speak Galilaeans? And how hear we every man in our own tongue, wherein we were born?" (Acts 2:1-8)

In this room, there were Jews from every nation. They spoke different languages. When the Holy Spirit who is the Spirit of Understanding according to Isaiah 11:2 came, communication was restored and they understood each other once again. These Jews came to keep the feast of Pentecost or (harvest) and they left with Jesus. The wisdom of God had planned for these men to be filled with the Holy Spirit so that when they went home, the gospel went with them. Suddenly God came upon them and almost immediately the gospel went into all the earth. These men came to keep the Law and they left with the Lawgiver and the one who fulfilled it living on the inside of them— not a bad trip. Literally, they came by themselves and left with God himself, that is radically good news. When God came in the building, the church left. There is a word for the modern church that is hell bent on getting God in the building when he wants to get us outside the building. Again, they came alone and left with Jesus, absolutely stunning. That is better than good news. That is amazing. The wisdom of God had this planned from before the foundation of the world. The times and seasons are in the Father's hand and he does what he wants when he wants, how he wants, and with who he wants because he can. God gives us the Holy Spirit so we can communicate with him and cooperate with him in his plan of redemption. The prophetic ministry plays a role in God's plan of redemption and we need to understand that role with clarity and precision so that we can do what is expected of us. Our stewardship in the Kingdom will be judged by what we have received, so it is crucial to understand what we have received. Everything we have received in the Kingdom was paid for by Christ Jesus on the tree. The issue is not when is Jesus going to return. The real issue is will we be doing what he commanded us to do when he returns. The revelation of urgency is supposed to produce faithfulness in us.

Understanding is what most people lack when it comes to fulfilling God's plan for their life. Most Christians' have a good heart to do God's will. It's usually a lack of spiritual understanding or an un-renewed mind that is not able to prove and identify the will of God. We need to clearly understand our role in the will of God. God will not do our job and we cannot do his. As we mature in faith, we grow in understanding. As much as we need power and authority we need wisdom and understanding. We expand the Kingdom of God with power and authority, but we legislate, govern and serve with wisdom and understanding. When wisdom grows up, it grows into understating. Wisdom is the application of revelation to make fruitful that which God has revealed. Understating is the last sentence. Understanding is a facilitator of purpose and destiny. Without understanding, people often wander spiritually instead of chartering a course and enjoying the ride. Often people don't have understating because they don't ask for it. Sometimes the only reason we have not is because we ask not. Being able to understand means we are able to mentally separate and connect all the dots. In Hebrew, one of the meanings of understanding is to mentally separate. In Hebrew, the culture was a culture of together. The children all learned together until they were ready to work. Here is something we need to understand. Learning should lead to action not just to us being more religious. In Greek one of the meanings of understanding is to put together. In the Greek culture, they did everything separately. (Here is an Old Testament and a New Testament verse where understanding means what was stated above: Nehemiah 8:8 and Acts 28:26.) Let me say it like this: the Kingdom is absolutely opposed to the culture. We need to understand God's ways especially if we want to co-labor with him. Just continue to walk by faith and pay attention to the Voice of God and you will surely grow in understanding.

Questions

1. Is understanding a must for us to faithfully steward what God has entrusted to us? Yes or No? Please explain.

_____

_____

_____

_____

2. Does faith come before understanding? Or does understanding give us faith?

_____

_____

_____

_____

3. How would your life change if you understood the circumstances you were in and why you were in them and what God was doing in the midst of it all? Explain.

_____

_____

_____

_____

Prayer of Impartation

Father in the name of Jesus let faith lead me to the place of understanding. Cause me to be faithful with all that you have entrusted to me. Let the Spirit of Understanding come and rest on me just like it did Jesus according to Isaiah 11:2.

Scriptures to Meditate On

• Job 6:24 *"Teach me, and I will hold my tongue: and cause me to understand wherein I have erred."*
• Proverbs 28:5 *"Evil men understand not judgment: but they that seek the LORD understand all things."*
• Daniel 10:11-12 *"And he said unto me, O Daniel, a man greatly beloved, understand the words that I speak unto thee, and stand upright: for unto thee am I now sent. And when he had spoken this word unto me, I stood trembling. Then said he unto me, Fear not, Daniel: for from the first day that thou didst set thine heart to understand, and to chasten thyself before thy God, thy words were heard, and I am come for thy words."*

Exercise

Here is an exercise that will help jump-start you to a new place of understanding. There are 24 hours in a day. Write down what you do in a normal 24-hour day. This will help you understand what you do. You will discover either your priorities are in order or they're not. One of the things about a maturing prophetic person is they have a high value for their time and truly desire to use it wisely. If you need to confess and repent go for it. Understanding what you do with your time will help you understand your priorities and your priorities will determine where you go in life. The right or wrong priorities mean you will either get or not get where you are going. If you are courageous you can do the same thing with the money you spend, which will help you understand another value system you have. Part of growing spiritually means we are willing to address some things in the natural that may be out of order. Order is what facilitates a sustainable blessing. Order is not religion, like "charismania" may teach you. I will give you something practical that I have come to understand. When paying off debt is not a serious priority, a financial breakthrough will be highly unlikely. Understanding where you are will help you understand how to position yourself properly for the future God intends for you, so listen carefully to his voice and obey.

Courage to Obey

(Adam LiVecchi)

courage |ˈkərij, ˈkə-rij|
noun
the ability to do something that frightens one:
• strength in the face of pain or grief: he fought his illness with great courage.
PHRASES
have the courage of one's convictions act on one's beliefs despite
danger or disapproval.
pluck up (or screw up or take) courage make an effort to do something that
frightens one.
take one's courage in both hands nerve oneself to do something that frightens one.
ORIGIN Middle English (denoting the heart, as the seat of feelings): from Old French
corage, from Latin cor 'heart.'

"There shall not any man be able to stand before thee all the days of thy life: as I was with Moses, so I will be with thee: I will not fail thee, nor forsake thee. Be strong and of a good courage: for unto this people shalt thou divide for an inheritance the land, which I sware unto their fathers to give them. Only be thou strong and very courageous, that thou mayest observe to do according to all the law, which Moses my servant commanded thee: turn not from it to the right hand or to the left, that thou mayest prosper whithersoever thou goest. This book of the law shall not depart out of thy mouth; but thou shalt meditate therein day and night, that thou mayest observe to do according to all that is written therein: for then thou shalt make thy way prosperous, and then thou shalt have good success. Have not I commanded thee? Be strong and of a good courage; be not afraid, neither be thou dismayed: for the LORD thy God is with thee whithersoever thou goest." (Joshua 1:5-9)

The word strong in verse 7 also means urgent, to seize, obstinate, and to behave self valiantly. This is the kind of leadership the body of Christ needs today. We should make decisions with the future in mind, but we still need to live urgently in the now. The word courage or courageous that is used here has several meanings, to be alert, to be steadfastly minded, or to prevail. Here God is commanding Joshua to obey the law and in obeying the law he would have to be strong and courageous. Obedience requires courage. Being courageous means moving forward into the unknown. It means moving forward into conflicts, which look more like impossibilities. The true Kingdom life is one of courage and of conflict. Courage is one of God's pre-requisites for leadership. People who change the world are courageous people. No one makes movies about losers; people always make movies about heroes. What usually makes a hero a hero is courage to act on behalf of another. Often compassion gives birth to courage. To bring change in the world both compassion and courage are necessary. Often we need some sort of courage for change because change involves risk. God was calling Joshua to lead the people of God into the promise land, but promise usually involves conflict. That is a good place to say amen.

A life of courage is one of purpose and destiny; it's a life of promise. Without courage there is no legacy for the next generation. Cowards can't leave a legacy for tomorrow if they live in fear today. When Moses died, Joshua became the leader of Israel. It took courage for Joshua to even begin to try to fill Moses' shoes or should I say sandals. Sometimes in life we need to have courage just to move forward and not live under the expectations of others. Many people live under the expectations of others. It's hard to have courage and be free to be strong when we live under the bondage of other people's low expectations of us. Sometimes we live under our own low expectations of ourselves. The renewed mind is a mind that thinks steadfastly and courageously. The greatest battle is not on the outside of us; it's actually on the inside of us.

The new heart and the new mind given to us in the New Covenant helps us to be strong in the Lord and courageous in following and obeying him. It will take courage to follow Jesus. In 2005, I was going into a communist country. A friend of mine and I were going there to preach Jesus and to get Bibles to people who needed them to continue their work in expanding the Kingdom. In many other countries, Bibles are so priceless because people actually do what they read, that is another message. Anyway we each had 76 Bibles to get into the country, a total of 152. They were in our suitcases and in our carry ons. This was such a time of redemption for me because just years ago I used to smuggle drugs from state to state, now I was smuggling Bibles for Jesus into a communist country. To be honest, I am not the most tough or courageous person by nature. This was Jesus in me. As I was going through customs and the customs agent in the communist country was looking at my passport, the Holy Spirit said, "Preach to him." In my head I am thinking Lord I am trying to get Bibles in here and this guy probably doesn't even speak English. In that moment I doubted my doubt and preached Jesus to this customs agent. It just so happened that he spoke English. As I was ministering to him, the Holy Spirit said to me "Give him a Bible." At that moment I took a deep breath opened my bag and gave him a Bible in his native language. He smiled at me stamped my passport and then we got our luggage and left. When I was going to get my luggage the Lord said to me, "Adam if you wouldn't have preached to that man no one would have." What God was saying to me is that it is important that we all play our part in his harvest. Other people's salvation is directly connected to our obedience. Remember our courage may very well be someone else's freedom from hell. There are people who risk their lives everyday for Jesus, so I am not saying that I am some sort of hero. I am just illustrating that to have courage we must step outside of our comfort zone. Courage grows in the secret place but is manifested as we follow and obey Jesus. In the world we live in it will take courage to follow Jesus. Courage is necessary if we are going to go anywhere in the Kingdom. The way of the Kingdom is the way of courage.

In 2006, my good friend Brandon Vajda and I went to a missions school called Holy Given at Life Center Church in Harrisburg, PA. Lesley-Anne Leighton was the leader of the school. She is one of the most radical believers I have ever met. Heidi Baker, Mel Tari, Charles Stock were just some of our teachers. Lesley-Anne has more boldness and courage than 99.8 % of any man I have ever met. I know some people will not like that statement, but it's true. Courage is not limited to men; courage is simply raw faith in motion. When people talk about woman not being able to minister, I think about Heidi Baker and Lesley-Anne Leighton, DR. Sandy Kirk, Patricia King, my wife, my mother and I just laugh at them. Remember religion always tries to oppress weaker people. Lesley-Anne is what the Bible speaks about concerning true Apostolic Ministry. Anyway one night at like 2:56 in the am the Lord said to me, "I want you and Brandon to go to Mexico." So the next day I asked Brandon if he wanted to go to Mexico; he said "yes" with no hesitation. There is a good prophetic lesson in this story. I didn't have to tell Brandon, "thus saith the Lord, we are going to Mexico." I just invited him and he came knowing it was the Lord. It's never good to try to manipulate someone's decision by using the Lord's name. There is a lot of manipulation and witchcraft with the name of Jesus attached to it but it has nothing to do with Jesus. Misusing the prophetic is a cowardly act. When people want to manipulate others, it's because they are profoundly insecure. Anyway, Brandon and I both knew no one in Mexico. We had no idea where we were going to stay or how we were going to get there or get back. Neither of us knew the language. This was outside of our comfort zone, but how in the world can we grow inside our comfort zone? Physically speaking it's only in breaking our comfort zone that our muscles get stronger, so it is with faith and courage. When Jesus said, "Come and follow me," he really meant it and he still means it today. The most prophetic thing we can do is follow Jesus.

Before we went to Mexico we were headed to the Azusa street 100-year centennial, celebrating the revival that happened with Rev. William Seymour. So we flew from New York to Los Angeles. Brandon forgot his iPod, which perhaps opened him up to talking to a man named Andres and his wife. They were business owners who lived in Southern California somewhere between LA and Tijuana Mexico. That man and his wife ended up having us in their house and taking us to Mexico in a BMW truck. He paid for our hotel and connected us to a Pastor in a bookstore in Tijuana named Guillermo. Two hours later we were preaching in his church. We stayed in the poor Pastor's house that had a house and a church in the hills of Tijuana, Mexico. It was a beautiful time; we loved every moment of it. The Pastor gave us his children's room, and had his children sleep in the room with him and his wife. It was very touching. The moment we stepped into his house, we felt like family. He knew how to receive strangers and turn them into family. It was just as courageous for him to receive us as it was for us to be in a country that we didn't speak the language or know where we were going to stay, or how we were going to get home. When we went to Mexico we cancelled our plane ticket home. Which literally meant we had no way to get home from Mexico. The Lord provided for us to take a bus through all the worst neighborhoods in America; it was an unforgettable journey. One man confessed to me on the bus that he murdered someone. Following Jesus involves going to more places than church on Sunday. The question I have for you is will you have the courage to follow Jesus and obey him. Will the church (you and I) have the courage to receive real disciples who really still follow Jesus today? When God wants to have mercy on cities, he sends true disciples. Will you be courageous enough to believe in the mercy of God especially for people and cities that don't deserve it?

The most courageous person ever to live was Jesus Christ. He got off a throne to be born into a manger only to be stretched out on a tree naked. He lived to die so that others may have eternal life in him. God is calling us to live in such a way, that others may have life even if it costs our very lives. God is looking for people who will count the cost and be willing to pay it to follow Jesus. We are to bring Jesus to places where people don't know him. We are called to be strong and very courageous.

"In the fear of the LORD is strong confidence: and his children shall have a place of refuge." (Proverbs 14:26)

Courage is about fearing God. If we have confidence on the inside, we will live courageously on the outside. The confidence is not in us but in Christ. He is our courage. The Holy Spirit desires to be our comforter but that is nearly impossible if we don't step out of our comfort zone. Remember to walk on water, we must have the courage to obey. If you want to walk on the water, you must step out of the boat. It's those who will be courageous and obey that will have testimonies of the Lord. Other people will have stories, but the ones with the testimonies will be the ones who had the courage to obey.

Questions

1. Is all fear bad?

_____

_____

_____

_____

2. Are you willing to let God make you a person who is courageous?

_____

_____

_____

_____

3. There is a difference between reckless and courageous. If you were filled with courage how would your life and the lives of those who are close to you change?

_____

_____

_____

_____

Prayer of Impartation

Father make me to be strong and very courageous. Lord give me the strength to follow you. Holy Spirit I invite you into every area of my life. Make me just like Jesus. Give me the courage to obey. I pray these things in Jesus' name.

Scriptures to Meditate On

• 2 Samuel 10:12 *"Be of good courage, and let us play the men for our people, and for the cities of our God: and the LORD do that which seemeth him good."*

• 1 Chronicles 28:20 *"And David said to Solomon his son, Be strong and of good courage, and do it: fear not, nor be dismayed: for the LORD God, even my God, will be with thee; he will not fail thee, nor forsake thee, until thou hast finished all the work for the service of the house of the LORD."*

• Psalm 27:13-14 *"I had fainted, unless I had believed to see the goodness of the LORD in the land of the living. Wait on the LORD: be of good courage, and he shall strengthen thine heart: wait, I say, on the LORD."*

Exercise

Ask the Holy Spirit how you can step out of your comfort zone. Spend some time listening to God and then act on what he says. It's not about a man made act of craziness that is recklessness. It's about a Holy Spirit led action. You will be strengthened to obey by his voice. The faith that is released in his voice will give you the courage to obey if you set your heart to obey before you hear from God. Courage for David was to fight Goliath. Courage for Daniel was to still pray in spite of the evil King's law. Courage for Jesus was to die on a tree. Courage to you and I is expressed in our obedience. If you want to go somewhere you haven't been before you may have to do something you haven't done before.

The Timing of God

(John Natale)

timing |ˈtīmiNG| keep definition just like it looks.
noun
the choice, judgment, or control of when something should be done: one of the secrets of golf is good timing.
• a particular point or period of time when something happens.
• (in an internal combustion engine) the times when the valves open and close, and the time of the ignition spark, in relation to the movement of the piston in the cylinder.

Many of us have wondered how and when the Timing of God comes or arrives in our lives. We often struggle with the worries of life and how we can get through each day. Prophetic words and prayers that have been offered don't always take the burden away. Yes, these are essential to our daily life but we must come to understand through wisdom and revelation that all things that come from God have a divine purpose and divine timing. Let me give you the definition of Timing.

Timing is everything. It gets us where we need to be at the right time and the right place. Without it, we are lost and on a road to destruction. Have you ever prayed for something and received it, but it just didn't feel right? Many times we find ourselves in situations where we feel prayers have been answered but still something does not feel right. In most cases, we have just been given what we have been asking and also begging for. We find that in the bible, where Israel is asking for a king and not appreciating what they have already. The King of the universe is with them. But they begged and begged and eventually got what they pleaded for. You can end up more distressed and confused than you were before if you get what you want at the wrong time. The Timing of God in our lives allows us to enter into the promises of Heaven when they are to be released over us and not when we demand them. It's like a well-oiled machine. When everything is functioning properly, all things work in sequence and in order. That is the biblical model of how we are to live our lives. Everything must be in order. Everything must be on time.

Below are some key scriptures that that show us how the Timing of God is spoken and influential in directing and the benefits it carries. I have found these scriptures to be most beneficial to me during times of doubt or discouragement. There are many times that we often choose the road of quick fixing rather than slow processing. Whenever you are in doubt regarding anything you are holding onto, remember that uncertainty leads to failure, while faith and confidence leads to victory.

• Isaiah 49:8 NKJV *"In an acceptable time I have heard and answered You, and in a day of salvation I have helped You; I will preserve You and give you as a covenant to the people, to restore the earth, to cause them to inherit the desolate moral wastes of heathenism, their heritages."*

• Psalm 31:15 NKJV *"My times are in Your hand; deliver me from the hands of my enemies, and those who persecute me."*

• Psalm 75:2 NKJV *"When I choose the proper time, for executing My judgments, I will judge uprightly says the Lord."*

Now let us look at some aspects of how the Timing of God actually pertains to everyday life. First, there is the submission that His will be done and not ours. When we try to do it our way we sometimes develop a "microwave" mentality. We want it now and we are not willing to accept anything else. So many people that have come across my path have a sense of urgency that their prayers must be answered immediately. We have become callous to the fact that the Lord is in control of all things. Discouragement and depression play a major role in this scenario. It's when your focus is on His eyes and your trust is put in His hand. Proverbs 3:5 NKJV says, *"Trust in the Lord with all of your heart and lean not on your own understanding, in all your ways acknowledge Him, and He shall direct your paths."*

Lazarus, I AM Coming!

We read that Jesus has been notified by His friends that Lazarus, His friend, is sick and in need of healing. We see and recognize that several elements of the timing of Jesus are demonstrated and cause the reader to reflect on his or her own life. First, we must ask ourselves what is the timing of God and how does it evolve in our lives? What are some of the attributes that affect our daily living? What causes delay and why does it sometimes come so easily?

Jesus was told to, "Come quickly Lord, your friend Lazarus is sick" but He was in no hurry to get there. The bible says that He actually stayed there two more days. We in our natural mind would have questioned that action and responded in a negative way, but there is a point that Jesus is trying to make. Faith in Him requires us to see in a realm that we are not accustomed to dwelling in for a lengthy period of time. Our inability to see ahead causes us to sometimes hit the panic button prematurely. Jesus stays back simply because he wants them to understand that when you call on Him, His response is not moved by man's desire, but the Father's.

Several keys that we see in response to His delay are the following:

Worry - Generated from fear.
Control - Generated from the need to control one's own life.
Doubt - Generated from lack of faith, but also contributed by past failures.
Discouragement - Generated from the inability see past your situation.
Blindness - Generated by the inability to see the power of God because of severity of the situation.
Deafness - Generated by the inability to hear the voice of God because of lack of sensitivity to the Holy Spirit.

Moving forward, the individual must come and recognize that the Holy Spirit speaks all the time to us. We are constantly being led in an arena of intimacy and conversation. It's just a matter of hearing and being sensitive to the things of Jesus. If we can remain in a posture of readiness, we can experience the wondrous works of Jesus in more ways than we can possibly imagine! That's why He even said to the disciples that, "It was for your own sake that I was not there." Their own faith, even the ones that were walking with Him, did not measure up to what was required for this situation. When He finally arrives, we see an incredible display of patience and expectancy. Yes, that is the word, expectancy.

Jesus is trying to teach the people that the key here is expectancy. He is in no rush simply because His timing is perfect. He knows what He is doing and there are no second bests, or plan B's. When Jesus gets to the tomb of Lazarus, He calls his name, "*Lazarus, come forth.*" Immediately, Lazarus appears and walks out. We see something very clearly in the text. Jesus is expecting him to arise, not hoping he would. So many times in our lives we deal with hope rather than expectancy. If we can just turn the corner and tap into that kind of thinking and living, we can experience breakthroughs that will seem to be effortless.

Here are the Keys to implement in your own life to understand God's Timing. When these are all running in your life, walking the path doesn't seem that hard; it just becomes a joyful journey and not a sorrowful road trip. Ask the Lord to reveal the things in your life that are holding you back and allow Him to implement the ingredients that are necessary to achieve greatness in your life. I hope this teaching on the Timing of God refreshes you and stirs you to move forward in supernatural ways and breakthroughs.

Faith
Submission
Intimacy
Expectancy
Sensitivity
Perseverance
Knowledge

Questions

1. How would you sum up your submission depth to the Lord? Have you completely surrendered your will?

_____

_____

_____

_____

2. Have you considered that Divine Timing is more important than fleshly desires?

_____

_____

_____

_____

3. What is the level of your expectation?

_____

_____

_____

_____

Prayer of Impartation

Jesus, I ask you to reveal and release your precious words to me. I ask you to open my mind and heart to see and understand your ways. Release fresh revelation and divine wisdom so that the needs and petitions are met and according to your perfect Timing, Release blessing that comes and overflows in more ways than one. Thank you for all you are and everything you do in their lives.

Scriptures to Meditate On

• Mark 13:33 NKJV *"Take heed, watch and pray; for you do not know when the time is."*

•Ecclesiastes 3:17 NKJV *"I said in my heart, God shall judge the righteous and the wicked, for there is a time for every purpose and for every work."*

• Psalm 119:126 NKJV *"It is time for you to act, oh Lord, for they have regarded Your law as void."*

• Luke 13:35 NKJV *"See! your house is left to you desolate; And assuredly, I say to you, you shall not see Me until the time comes when you shall say, "Blessed is He who comes in the name of the Lord!"*

• Acts 1:7 NKJV *And He said to them, "It is not for you to know times or seasons which the Father has put in His own Authority."*

• Hebrews 4:16 NKJV *"Let us therefore come boldly draw to the throne of grace, that we may obtain mercy and find grace to help in time of need appropriate help and well-timed help, coming just when we need it."*

Exercise

Lift up your heart to Jesus and ask Him to completely fill you up with His love and strength. Release your will and surrender everything to Him. Meditate on the word day and night and seek the will of the Father and trust and obey. Pray 20 minutes and ask Holy Spirit how you should adjust your timing.

Prophetic Faithfulness

(John Natale)

faithfulness |ˈfāTHfəlnəs|
the quality of being faithful; fidelity: faithfulness in marriage.

What an opportunity God granted to Jonah in His mercy. This was like a mulligan in golf. It was an opportunity to replay the shot and record a better score but with eternal consequences in the lives of many people. God had not discarded Jonah because of his failure. He was still merciful to allow him the privilege of ministry. Prophetically, today we have the same expectations from God that were given to Jonah. We also receive the same mercy. There is a requirement that God gives us, and that is to speak the truth. Throughout history the word of God has not changed, yet some believe that the role of the prophet has changed. Teaching has become calloused and weak. Many believe that it is merely required to just encourage and exhort. This is false. Prophets have been called not just to encourage, but to speak truth. This is and will always be a standard in our living. Prophetic Faithfulness is merely the desire and willingness to release the word of the Lord individually or corporately. As the definition clearly states, true to one's word, promises or vows. Prophetically, this offers the individual the ability to speak truth to one's own future and destiny. Truth changes lives. Truth sets people free. Truth enables destiny. Your prophetic position helps someone else align themselves correctly with their prophetic promise. Have you ever thought about how you can change a life just by the way you position yourself? Remember that everything you do and say has an effect in someone's life.

Jonah spent much of his time dealing with his will and not God's. He wants to deliver the message but he wants to deliver it the way he wants to. The right attitude and heart of compassion causes us to release goodness and gentleness. Kind of like the way Jesus speaks. The purpose of this chapter is to understand how and why we deliver the goods the way we are expected to. The main emphasis of the book of Jonah is God's desire to change the heart of His people so that our love towards the lost reflects His heart of compassion and mercy. Prophetically, this is how we obtain the mercy and grace in our life. He has so much patience with us. We have so little patience with others. Can we be the people that He so desires? Yes, we can.

The preaching of God's prophetic message of imminent judgment can change the hearts of men and turn away the impending wrath of God. This is so critical because timing is everything. You have a specific directive that must be carried out. The question is, are you willing to deliver the goods?

God Calls His Prophet a Second Time

"Now the word of the Lord came to Jonah the second time, saying "Arise, go to Nineveh, that great city, and preach to it the message that I tell you." (Jonah 3:1-2 NKJV)

He is the God of the Second Chance; but don't take advantage of His patience. He will not always give you chance after chance.Has the discipline of God, the trials that God has brought into your life because of tests, made you more obedient or less obedient to him? In the long haul have you become more flexible or less flexible in responding to God's heart desires? Are you more submissive to his will or less submissive? Has the stress made you bitter toward God, or better in serving him and following him? Are you more consistent in running away from him or agreeing with him? Examine yourself right now and be real. Where are you at?

God commands faithfulness in Proclaiming His Message. Jonah 1:2 NKJV states, *"Arise, go to Nineveh the great city and cry out against it; for their wickedness has come up before me."* God doesn't always give you the entire picture up front. He only requires you to act on what He is releasing at that time. There are times that He will not give you everything you are asking for upfront. That reason is because if He does, the enemy now knows everything as well and he will most definitely act on it and try to persuade you to have a change of heart. Many times the task at hand seems greater than we are expecting. God casts a big vision of great challenge and great compassion as seen in Jonah 3:3 NKJV, *"So Jonah arose and went to Nineveh according to the word of the Lord. Now Nineveh was an exceedingly great city, a three-*

day journey in extent."

The Mission
Starting the Journey and Speaking the Truth

Tackling the scope of the mission is the hardest part and it's actually the beginning. Conveying the urgency of the mission is the next step that usually brings the testing of are you really going to go through with it? Proclaiming the message of the mission is unpopular and dangerous. The word of judgement that God wanted to deliver through Jonah, "*Yet forty days, and Nineveh shall be overthrown*" may have not been very popular. (Jonah 3:4 NKJV) However this short message was exactly what Nineveh needed. Short sermons can be quite effective. Not only are they straight to the point, they get the attention of the individual you are speaking to. They will expose what you are made of and how you respond to critical situations that are potentially life-threatening.

The Movement
Humbling Themselves and Petitioning God for Forgiveness

Perhaps most impressive and astonishing of all time is an entire city repenting and turning away from their wickedness and going back to God. What inspired such a dramatic turnaround? God's heart of love and compassion reaching out to them inspired the turnaround. It came from the unusual circumstances of the unusual prophet. The response of the people was a shock to the man of God.

Corporate movement towards repentance on the part of all the people humbling themselves before God caused them to react in the correct way.

"So the people of Nineveh believed God, claimed a fast, and put on sackcloth, from the greatest to the least of them." (Jonah 3:5 NKJV)

Your pursuit of God involves confession of sin and petitioning God for mercy. There is no caste system when it comes to our standing before God. The response of the King Nineveh is that of a personal response same as that of the people. Jonah 3:6 NKJV states, "*When the word reached the king of Nineveh, he arose from his throne, laid aside his robe from him, covered himself with sackcloth, and sat on the ashes."* The effectiveness of Jonah's preaching was that his words reached the king. The king now has chosen to take on a leadership position invoking his authority and partners with God. He called for an extreme expression of humility, as well as commanding repentance and petitioning God for Mercy. Jonah 3:7-9 NKJV states, *"And he caused it to be proclaimed and published throughout Nineveh by the decree of the king and his nobles: But both man and beast must be covered with sackcloth and let men call on God earnestly that each may turn from his wicked way and from the violence which is in his hands. Who can tell if God will turn and relent, and turn away from His fierce anger, so that we may not perish?"* Here we see that the faithfulness of Jonah and his urgency causes reaction in the hearts of men and true revelation to be exposed in their hearts. The fear of God coupled with hope in His mercy causes the individual to submit and yield to the will of the Father. It will humble you, fast.

These are some key questions that will help you in the process of being Prophetically Faithful. Not only will they help you help others, but they will help develop and nurture your very being. It will expose your weaknesses and your strengths. Your character will shine like a light in a dark place and your heart will be shaped and molded to the very likeness of Jesus.

Questions

1. Do you have compassion towards others?

_____

_____

_____

_____

2. Do you see others the way Jesus sees them?

_____

_____

_____

_____

3. How do you tolerate sin?

_____

_____

_____

_____

4. Are you afraid of speaking truth?

_____

_____

_____

_____

5. Do you run from confrontation?

_____

_____

_____

_____

Prayer of Impartation

Holy Spirit, I ask you to touch the heart and reveal your heart to me. I ask you to give me the revelation of your eyes. Allow me to see through the eyeglasses of eternity. To see how you see people, to feel what you feel and to love the way you love. I ask that your Spirit release a fire to blaze inside and cause an urgency in my heart to speak truth and be the voice that you have called me to be.

Scriptures to Meditate On

• Jonah 1:10 NKJV *"For the men knew that he fled from the presence of the Lord, because he had told them."*

Many times in our lives we run from the Lord because we know that we are expected to release truth. Fear sets in and binds us because of several key ingredients. One is rejection and the other is disappointment. We concern ourselves with acceptance and affirmation. Always trying to run from the truth and not willing to give to others what has been spoken to us. If we would just trust in the Lord and not lean on our own understanding, all would be all right. Does that ring a bell? Your fear does not just hinder and alter your life but it also affects the life and or lives you are called to help.

• Jonah 4:10 NKJV *"But the Lord said, "You have had pity on the plant for which you have not labored, nor made it grow, which came up in a night and perished in a night."*

There are times that we moan and complain about things that are not even worth talking about or giving any time for. We choose to live in the realm of excuses and try anything to get out of what we have been directed to do. Jonah has chosen to have more compassion for a plant rather than having compassion for people. Prophetic Faithfulness is a substance that comes from the heart of the King. All things that are spoken to us and ordered to release to others come from the heart of love. This chapter is all about understanding the simple principal of caring for others and not just yourself.

• Jonah 4:11 NKJV *"And should I not pity Nineveh, that great city, in which are more than one hundred and twenty thousand persons who cannot discern between their right and their left-and much livestock?"*

This scripture is a great example of why Voices in the Wilderness | School of the Prophets was birthed. It helps teach people to hear the voice of God and act on it. The Lord gives a great example to Jonah that the people can't distinguish right from wrong. His desire is to send a messenger to lost people and heal the hearts of broken people. That is why we are called to advance the Kingdom of God. To be the voice that is crying out in the wilderness we must prepare the way of the Lord.

• Jonah 4:6 NKJV *"And the Lord prepared a plant and made it come up over Jonah, that it might be shade for his head to deliver him from his misery."*

Can we understand why this has happened? Now put yourself in Jonah's shoes and try to relate. Many jump to conclusions regarding the plant. God purposely made the plant to teach him a lesson. Compassion for Jonah was released but also chastisement as well. Have you ever been comforted by the Lord and then at the same time feel like everything just went bad? I'm sure Jonah did not have a clue about what was going on. Just like many times in our life we experience the same situation But in the end, we always come out better than when we first started. The love of the Lord is good and never ends. It never fails and is never too early or too late.

Exercise

Pray in the Spirit and ask the Lord to show you certain individuals that He wants you to speak to. Pray for 20 minutes and meditate on the scriptures about the Great Commission (Mark 16:15-18, Matthew 28:18-20).

Warriors of the Prophetic

(John Natale)

warrior |ˈwôrēər|
noun
(esp. in former times) a brave or experienced soldier or fighter.
ORIGIN Middle English: from Old Northern French werreior, variant of Old
French guerreior, from guerreier 'make war,' from guerre 'war.'

In this chapter, I am teaching the principles of the Prophetic Warrior. There are many times in our life and especially during the time of our prophetic journey that battles arise. How we handle these battles are critical in every aspect of your walk and the decisions you make along the way. I am a firm believer that all believers will go through testing that at times will prove them to the core. As our faith grows and our authority increases, so do the tests. Some of us like to call them battles. I myself am a battlefield veteran. Not only do we spend a lot of time on the battlefield, but our advancement has come through victories and defeats. One of the keys that I would like to introduce you to is fearlessness. This is one of the most important character traits a believer must carry in order to be victorious. Fearlessness enables you to move forward and take over ground. It allows you to lead and not follow. Let's look at an example. David saw Goliath and the havoc he was causing. At such a young age, he should have been intimidated and overwhelmed with fear, but with an intense relationship with his God, he knew who he was. He knew what was inside of him and most of all, he knew what the consequences were for not moving forward. Battlefields are a central part of our life and will always be. They will never stop and will always increase as your journey expands. Many people that I come in contact with are actually afraid of the enemy and keep a low profile from him. When they engage in the fight, they operate on the defensive rather than the offensive. The enemy has one thing that is his target, and that is intimidation. Many times believers don't want to be tested simply because it will cost you something. I have always believed that if you want to see great signs and wonders, then you will go through great testing to see what you are made of. If you want to see a town, region or nation shaken by the power of God, then you better be prepared to be shaken yourself.

There are various types of battlefields, but what we are discussing now is the field that comes with your prophetic journey. Are you willing to go? Are you willing to lay down your life. At what price do you draw the line? If you are reading this manual, then you are most likely an individual that is crying out for more and wants to be used by God to the fullest. The scenario that has always made an impact in my life and always stood out the most is when David sees Goliath and runs at him. What an amazing display of courage and warrior spirit. Now I would like you to understand a very serious position. In order for you to experience the greater glory, you must be hungry for the things of God, but you must also be thirsty. David was thirsty for the greater things of his God. He desired to experience the heart in a unique way. Now let's look at the second key to moving forward as a warrior. David knew he had a great calling on his life. He could not operate in the way he did or respond the way he did to unless his inner being was that of unusual proportion. He was created to fight, conquer and rule. That's what each and every one of us is capable of doing. The determination and expectation of his mindset changed everything around him. Your mindset is to be just the same. Did you know that there is power in your words? If you are not blessing then you are cursing. You can have what you say if you believe in it enough. Why was David so fierce and confident at such a young age? Many times the battles that come our way are so intimidating that we run from them. It's amazing that the natural things in life can actually dominate us and dictate our future. One principle that you must remember and never forget is this; the spiritual realm is more a reality than the natural realm. Many people have a hard time with this scenario, but when you think about it, everything is spirit led or breathed and manifests in the natural. Jesus only did what He saw His Father doing and spoke only what His Father was saying. We are to follow that golden rule. If we stay in that parameter, we are in the safe zone. David operated in this chemistry. Why he was so victorious is because he understood the equation of winning. Have you figured out the equation in your life?

God knows that Satan is going to be loosed on the earth for his last hour of warfare. And the Lord is going to need well-trained warriors who will prevail over all the powers of hell. Right now he is doing a quick work in His remnant; it is called crisis training. This kind of training requires believers like you and me to be physically disciplined as well as spiritually. Here is a scripture to think about; Jacob threw his whole body into the battle, all his human ability. A fighting spirit had risen up in him and Hosea 12:3 NKJV says, *"In his strength he struggled with God." This verse has great meaning for all who want to prevail in prayer. It says Jacob won the battle "in his strength."* If you are going to prevail in these last days, you are going to have to put all your body and strength into it.

A few years ago while ministering in Pennsylvania, my family and I had the opportunity to visit The Battlefield of Gettysburg. I was blown away by the presence of God that I felt on the land. At one particular moment while I was praying, I was caught up in the spirit and I actually felt the blood of those that gave their lives for our justice. Many do not know that there were so many soldiers that were fighting for a cause that they did not know. The one thing they had was the desire and commitment to defend their country. The two groups fighting, the Union and the Confederate had many followers of Jesus. Not many people think about that. Just imagine fighting on a battlefield and the individual across the field from you is also a believer. Do you keep fighting or do you drop your weapon? We as believers get so caught up in the natural battlefields of life and throw in the towel so quickly. There is no weapon pointed in your face or a bayonet being thrusted in your side. These men were made out of the mold of courage and fearlessness. I was deeply moved on how there was so much pain and hardship that accompanied that time. They all shared common value as we do.

Fight the good fight and never give up. Friend, never give up. There is a world out there that needs you to engage in the fight—to be an overcomer. I want to share some words that have inspired me throughout the years. I know they will speak to your spirit. In a book called; God Bless America, James Kennedy writes these truly inspiring words, "My great passion for America is twofold; first, that every believer would be absolutely faithful to the Great Commission; and then, that every believer would take seriously the challenge to reclaim this nation for Christ. If we become engaged and if we carry out the "cultural mandate" of the church, then there is no reason that we cannot reclaim our heritage of faith and freedom and see this nation renewed." What an amazing speech! That sums it all up. The battlefield you are fighting in does not just impact yours, but it impacts many. Remember this day in your life. Everything you are doing whether you have been beaten down or are standing at the top of the mountain is touching someone's life in a big way!

Questions

1. Is your battlefield natural or spiritual?

_____

_____

_____

_____

2. Are you fighting in your own strength or the Lord's?

_____

_____

_____

_____

3. Are you a person that wants to be in the front lines? If so, why?

_____

_____

_____

_____

4. Do you run from battles?

_____

_____

_____

_____

5. Are you willing to lay down your life for another?

_____

_____

_____

_____

6. Do you know that battles are part of God's plan for your life?

_____

_____

_____

_____

7. Are you teachable? Are you willing to learn from others?

_____

_____

_____

_____

Prayer of Impartation

Lord I ask you to reveal your plans for me. Release a warrior spirit like David's in my life. Cause me to be stirred up to engage in the battle and prophesy like David did regarding Goliath. Cause me to speak to my mountain and be thou removed. Let the fire of God be released on me and make me as bold as a lion. In these last days, cause in me a fiery soldier to come forth that has no fear but is filled with power and authority that can only come from you. In your precious name, Jesus.

Scriptures to Meditate On

• Luke 10:19 NKJV *"Behold, I give you the authority to trample on serpents and scorpions, and over all the power of the enemy, and nothing shall by any means hurt you."*

• Luke 9:1 NKJV *"Then He called His twelve disciples together and gave them power and authority over all demons, and to cure diseases."*

• Mark 6: 7,13 NKJV *"And He called the twelve to Him, and began to send them out two by two, and gave them power over unclean spirits ... And they cast out many demons, and anointed with oil many who were sick, and healed them."*

• Matthew 10:1 NKJV *"And when He had called His twelve disciples to Him, He gave them power over unclean spirits, to cast them out, and to heal all kinds of sickness and all kinds of disease."*

• Matthew 10:6-8 NKJV *"But go rather to the lost sheep of the house of Israel. And as you go, preach, saying, 'The kingdom of heaven is at hand.' Heal the sick, cleanse the lepers, raise the dead, cast out demons. Freely you have received, freely give."*

• Isaiah 54:17 NKJV *"No weapon formed against you shall prosper, and every tongue which rises against you in judgment you shall condemn. This is the heritage of the servants of the Lord, and their righteousness is from me," says the Lord."*

• Psalm 44:5 NKJV *"Through You we will push down our enemies; through Your name we will trample those who rise up against us. For I will not trust in my bow, nor shall my sword save me. But You have saved us from our enemies, and have put to shame those who hated us. In God we boast all day long, and praise Your name forever."*

• 2 Chronicles 16:9 NKJV *"For the eyes of the Lord run to and fro throughout the whole earth, to show Himself strong on behalf of those whose heart is loyal to Him."*

Exercise

Now I want you to pray in the spirit and seek the Lord. Can you think of anything that you might be running from? Are there any battles that have intimidated you? If so, engage in the Spirit right now and ask for revelation on how to react and respond. Pray, ask for wisdom and act. Don't be afraid to engage in the fight. A true warrior hits his target head-on. Meaning, don't run but be on the offensive. Minister to someone tonight, pray for someone tonight and most of all, press in more tonight and sacrifice your time. In the end, Jesus gets all the glory and you have just advanced the gospel.

Prophetic Harvest

(John Natale)

harvest |ˈhärvist|
noun
the process or period of gathering in crops: helping with the harvest.
• the season's yield or crop: a poor harvest.
• the product or result of an action: in terms of science, Apollo yielded a meager
harvest.

In this chapter, I will discuss the importance of how the prophetic is used and how not to be used for the harvest. Is it possible that the prophetic can actually be used in a negative way? The answer to that question is yes. But first, we will look at how it is implemented into one's life the correct way and how it used in the most beneficial way. Have you ever wanted to witness to someone but just got tired of handing out the same old tracks or reading someone else's handouts? There is a tool that is extremely successful and you have the capability of carrying around, what I call is the Prophetic Toolbag! Prophetic evangelism is simply being led by the Holy Spirit like in the book of Acts where it is common to be Spirit-led in physical directions, towards specific people and be given specific wisdom of what to do or say.

"But you shall receive power when the Holy Spirit has come upon you; and you shall be witnesses to Me in Jerusalem, and in all Judea and Samaria, and to the ends of the earth." (Acts 1:8-10 NKJV)

Prophetic evangelism is also when the Holy Spirit gives believers the revelation or insight concerning the not-yet believer's past or present circumstances through words of knowledge. The Holy Spirit also gives insight into their future through the gift of prophecy.

"Pursue love, and desire spiritual gifts, but especially that you may prophesy."
(Corinthians 14:1 NKJV)

The words of knowledge given to a believer during a time of evangelism opens up the heart of a person who does not yet know God. When this happens, the person's heart is usually broken open to a place where love can pour in. Often times, they are convinced of God's love for them and they often immediately make a decision to become a follower of Jesus Christ. The first key to prophetic evangelism is sensitivity to the Spirit of God. You must first pray and listen to the voice of God in order to release what He is saying. The second key is compassion. In order to successfully minister to a person, there must be a love for the lost. The third key is boldness. There must be a willingness and fearless mind-set to deliver the truth. You must not be worried or concerned about how the individual responds in the situation. If all three of these keys are implemented in you life, your evangelistic experiences will not just be rewarding to you but the eternal rewards for the recipient will be priceless.

Now let us discuss the ramifications of prophetic evangelism without these three keys. First, many times people speak to those on the streets, mall, workplaces, and etc. So often, conversation starts and there is no prayer involved or sensitivity to the Spirit of God. This causes an immediate red flag. Why, because you are now speaking from the flesh and not from the voice of God. It is very hard to do what God commanded us when we try to do it without him. Here is the scripture that Jesus speaks on how we are all to follow. *"Then Jesus answered and said to them, Most assuredly, I say to you, the Son can do nothing of Himself, but what He sees the Father do; for whatever He does, the Son also does in like manner."* (John 5:19 NKJV)

Second, when the individual that is ministering does not have compassion or love for the lost, there is the common denominator of ridicule, debate and offense. Often when a conversation has started, and this attribute is missing, debates usually occur because the words that are being released are not anointed and do not bring life, but judgment and condemnation. Third, is the lack of boldness or fear. Many individuals do not even consider evangelism simply because they are afraid of the response they will get. They have a fear of rejection and a fear that they are not knowledgeable enough to speak the right words in the scenario they are in. When this practice is performed incorrectly, the end result is discouragement and failure. When the practice is performed correctly, the end result is satisfaction and joyful.

Now let's talk about Revival. It is not, is a three-day event that we advertise as "Revival." We do not bring revival. Ministries do not bring revival. It's not a state of mind, but a state of impact that drastically changes the moral climate of an area and region. The way people think in that region changes. The way people treat each other changes. The fog of deception begins to lift and the "eyes of their understanding are enlightened." Revival is an experience not a definition. It can't be created or copied. It can only be demonstrated by radical obedience of those who pursue it. It deals with people, not statistics. Revival starts in the heart of the individual. Revival does not look like we expect it to look. Revival is shocking. It never dresses the same, never smells the same; it's unorthodox. It's unreligious. It surprises; it's hardly ever invited or expected. It comes on its own terms and in its own way. It comes suddenly, and it doesn't always wear the face we expect. It will show up when you least expect it and most of the time it comes to completely stretch you and make your world uncomfortable. It comes and sits at our feet and begs for a piece of bread. It demands more than we have to give. It demands God.

Revival is waiting for us on the streets. It's calling to us from foreign fields and obscure places. It's crying and yearning for even one person who will rise from the confines of normality and pursue it. It's a person who will approach the throne of grace with boldness and expect a miracle. Revival is a fire, and souls are the wood that keeps the fire burning.

We are the catalysts of this fire. We are the gatekeepers who must cry out, *"Here am I send me!"* (Isaiah 6:8 NKJV). Revival is not a hand on a clock waiting for the alarm to sound. It's the ever-beating heart of every person who has a passion for people. It's that hope of glory, Christ in us. Once we begin to step into the realm of life that is not about us, then, we'll begin to see His power unmatched. It's through our hands that He desires to demonstrate His glory. It's through our mouth that He longs to release His personality. We are revival.

The next great move of God will be seen in the streets. But this time, it will be a move of God that is not common and no one can put his or her name on it. Harvest is experienced only in the open air with the hot sun and the cool evening breeze. Its abundance usually comes forth through sweat and effort. Harvest is outside. Harvest is where the people are. The church harvest is upon us. Harvest is most surely upon us. Here is a famous line from a movie that has changed my life. It comes from the movie, Field of Dreams. It goes like this, " They will come; they will most definitely come." This line has changed my life simply because it spoke about people coming to a field wanting to see a game. They had no idea why they were coming; they just knew they had to come, and they were willing to go wherever and whenever to get there. That is revival. It causes the individuals to go after God in a way that is desperation and hunger in its highest form.

Questions

1. How would you rate your compassion level for the lost?

_____

_____

_____

_____

2. Do you have a passion for people?

_____

_____

_____

_____

3. When was the last time you witnessed to someone?

_____

_____

_____

_____

4. Are you dealing with any fear in your life regarding speaking to others?

_____

_____

_____

_____

5. Do you have rejection issues?

_____

_____

_____

_____

Prayer of Impartation

Lord I ask you to fill up your servant to overflowing. Release a fire for the lost. Release a passion for people that is unquenchable. Allow them to see what you see and impart a compassion to speak life and be used to heal the sick, heal the broken hearted to those that are bound and lost. Stir them up so they can be used in so many ways that will bring glory to your name.

Scriptures to Meditate On

• Numbers 11:29 NKJV *"Then Moses said to him, Are you zealous for my sake? Oh that all the Lord's people were prophets and that the Lord would put his spirit upon them."*

• Joel 2:28 NKJV *"And it shall come to pass afterward That I will pour out My spirit upon all flesh, and the sons and your daughters shall prophesy. Your old men shall dream dreams and your young men shall see visions."*

• Mark 16:15 NKJV *"go into all the world and preach the gospel to every creature."*

• Matthew 9:37-38 NKJV *"Then he said to his disciples, The harvest is truly plentiful but the laborers are few. Therefore pray the Lord of the harvest, to send out laborers into His harvest."*

• Matthew 28:18-20 NKJV *"And Jesus came and spoke to them, saying, "All authority has been given to Me in heaven and on earth. Go therefore and make disciples of all the nations, baptizing them in the name of the Father and of the Son and of the Holy Spirit, teaching them to observe all things that I have commanded you. And lo, I am with you always, even to the end of the age."*

• Luke 19:10 NKJV *"For the Son of Man has come to seek and to save that which was lost."*

• Acts 1:8 NKJV *"But you shall receive power when the Holy Spirit has come upon you; and you shall be witnesses to Me in Jerusalem, and in all Judea and Samaria, and to the end of the earth."*

• Acts 2:38 NKJV *"The Peter said to them, Repent, and let every one of you be baptized in the name of Jesus Christ for the remission of sins; and you shall receive the gift of the Holy Spirit."*

• Acts 3:19 NKJV *"Repent therefore and be converted, that your sins may be blotted out, so that times of refreshing may come from the presence of the Lord."*

• Acts 4:12 NKJV *"Nor is there salvation in any other, for there is no other name under heaven given among men by which we must be saved."*

• Romans 10:9-10 NKJV *"That if you confess with your mouth, the Lord Jesus and believe in your heart that God has raised him from the dead, you will be saved. For with the heart one believes unto righteousness, and with the mouth confession is made unto salvation."*

Exercise

Pray in the spirit and ask the Lord to show you loved ones that are lost. Pray and ask how you can be used to touch lives. The next time you see people, ask the Lord to give you boldness to speak to them. Pray for people who need a physical healing in their body. This can be done outside the home or on the streets or even at work if possible. Call friends or family members in need of salvation or healing and pray with them over the phone. Lay your hands on your body if you need a healing and prophesy to your situation. Study the scriptures that speak and teach on healing. Remember to pray and give God all you got! It will all be worth it.

The Process of the Journey

(John Natale)

process 1 | ˈprä͵ses, ˈpräsəs, ˈprō-|
noun
1 a series of actions or steps taken in order to achieve a particular end: military operations could jeopardize the peace process.
• a natural or involuntary series of changes: the aging process.

Hearing the Word, Trusting the Promise, Seeing the Breakthrough

Have you ever thought about your journey? Have you thought about where your journey leads and what you have to go through to get where you believe you are destined for? Sure you have, but what about the process? In this chapter, I am going to teach you some fundamentals on the decisions, experiences and challenges that come your way during the most exciting time of your life—The Journey.

First I want to talk about hearing the word over your life. Faith comes by hearing and hearing by the word of God. The initial step to any process is hearing. You must be able to hear in order to react. What we are determined to do with this manual is to help people hear the voice of God clearly and step into their destiny or calling. Now let us look at a passage and see how it parallels with the everyday believer.

"Now it came to pass after these things that God tested Abraham, and said to him, Abraham! And he said, Here I am. Then He said, Take now your son, your only son Isaac, whom you love, and go to the land of Moriah and offer him there as a burnt offering on one of the mountains of which I shall tell you." (Genesis 22:1-2 NKJV)

Abraham had no idea that a test of this measure was about to knock on his door. Remember, he was given a promise that his descendants were to be of enormous proportions. This promise puts him in expectation mode waiting for the word of the Lord to come to fruition. Can you relate to this? I know I can. We all have been given words from the Lord that we are waiting on. But let's keep going further. He hears the word and now the second step is his reaction. His reaction to this scenario can make him or break him. We all know by reading the text that Abraham chooses to obey the Lord and offer him up as a sacrifice. Do you know how hard it must have been for this man of God to move forward? The element that stands out the most is his faith in God. We at times have heard the Holy Spirit speak to us and ask us to carry out certain things that may have been hard to swallow or completely comprehend. And at times we have not obeyed and carried out the plans. Fear sets in and we crumble under the pressure. But what we are learning here is the ability to hear and obey through faith. When you have seen His eyes, heard His voice and felt His love, nothing gets in the way or hinders progress. Abraham had a relationship with his God that was unmovable by man. He had a trust that was unshakeable and irreversible. This is where you must ask yourself the same question. Have there been situations in your life that you knew you responded incorrectly? We all know that the choice is yours; you either accept or reject it. There must be a distinguishing factor that separates spiritual from natural thinking. If you spend most of your time trying to figure things out and break down and analyze everything that is set before you, you will bear fruit that is small and weak in substance. Remember, the spiritual realm is far greater of a reality than the natural realm. We look at our present state of circumstances instead of seeing through the eyes of Jesus and what He sees. It's time to replace those old worn out glasses and with some Holy Spirit prescription contact lenses. They are always clear and they are much easier on the soul.

Now let's explore trusting the promise over your life. There are times in our life when trials come that will test you and expose your weaknesses and strengths. During the course of these encounters, there are specific hot spots that are targeted. We will now look at these in sequence. First is character. This is tested to shape your integrity, love, compassion and so on. Testing is allowed simply because it makes you more Christ-like. Second is depth. Depth tests how much you are willing to give up and how much you are capable of handling. Third is ownership. This tests how much you control your own situation and how much you are willing to let go of and release or surrender your will. Fourth is love. Love tests how deep your love goes and where its boundaries are and if there are any conditions or requirements that are unconditional.

In Genesis 22:2, we learn that Abraham is given a test to determine his depth of trust. Trusting in all your situations is not the easiest thing to carry out but we must come to understand that Jesus will have His way in our life and there is no way around that. Faith is the substance of things hoped for, the evidence of things not seen (Hebrews 11:1). We are also told that we need only to have faith of a mustard seed. Jesus sends His tests to see if we are still making Him the central focus of our life. Prophetically, trusting the promise is easier said than done. Holding onto a promise that has been prophetically given shows great depth and faith. You are actually believing in something that you have not seen or and you don't have evidence that it will actually come into existence. That's the amazing aspect of the prophetic. It releases future mysteries and deposits them in the present. All you need is a set of eyes to see and a pair of ears to hear. It's that simple; it's that easy. Hunger and desperation to have the mind of Christ
is foundational to the prophetic.

Now we will examine the grand finale of the Journey: Seeing the Breakthrough. This is where we contend for our breakthrough and actually see it come to fruition in our lives. First, I would like to display the attitude of Abraham during his time on the mountain. As he finished his journey to the top of the hill, he prepared an altar for a sacrifice. Isaac was that sacrifice. Here he makes choices that do not even make sense in the natural. He shows strength that is physically impossible and faith that is unsurpassed by anything that is commonly dealt with today. He was about to sacrifice his son and through a prophetic promise, he was willing to go to the very edge of the envelope to see it come to pass. Many have questioned whether or not Abraham actually believed that he would actually carry out such a task, but the text does not give us that hidden mystery. What it does tell you is the simple fact that he was intimate with his God and he trusted everything that was spoken to him. At the most critical time during his contention, the Angel of the Lord appears and says, "Abraham, stay your hand, now I know that you fear God." (Genesis 22:12) Do you see here how the Lord waits at times for the last critical moment to release blessing and of course answers? Many times that has been the story of our life. The 11th hour. He is never late and always right on time! The breakthrough was the ram that was caught in the thicket. It actually followed him up the mountain but it was on the other side. That's what is so amazing about how the Lord works with us. Even when we do not see what we are fighting for, it is walking right along side of us. We just are not allowed to see it until the kairos moment of time.

Abraham's faith was so strong that nothing could shake or change it. This is where we need to be. How you get there has been dictated in this chapter. How you end up is all up to you? Abraham's whole journey carried all the bullet points we have gone over in this segment. Now we need to apply them and walk the journey that has been calling your name since the beginning of time. Remember, the word over your life does not just focus on the blessing, but causes you to embrace Jesus even more. Abraham also was taught that everything belongs to God. Nothing is yours. Isaac carries the wood like Jesus. He walks up a hill to be laid down and to die. This is a symbolic to Jesus laying down His life for the redemption on sin. Isaac was being laid down to test love and be used to fulfill a promise of seed. So when you examine all of these points that we have discussed, it is very clear that tests are not given to see failure, but they are administered to produce blessing that is greater than you can possibly imagine. In closing, look back and carefully study these points. You will grow in an ever-increasing knowledge and revelation on the prophetic promises that are in covenant with you. Contend until you have seen breakthrough and watch the harvest come forth and overtake you. It's just around the corner; it just might be caught in the thicket as well!

From Genesis to Jesus speaking in John 3:16, we are consumed with Love, Trust, and Promise.

Questions

1. Have you ever considered that your journey is one that you are not in control of?

_____

_____

_____

_____

2. Are you willing to go down a road where you do not see the outcome?

_____

_____

_____

_____

3. Can you sacrifice your desires for someone else's destiny?

_____

_____

_____

_____

4. If you were asked, could you travel a road alone?

_____

_____

_____

_____

5. How much are you willing to let go of to see prophetic promise come to fruition?

_____

_____

_____

_____

Prayer of Impartation

Lord I ask you to open up the Heavens in my life. Show me that the prophetic journey is one that brings peace, joy, and victory. Release breakthrough and justice to me as I hold onto the covenant promise that has been spoken over my life. I speak forth that my destiny will not be hindered or voided out, but will manifest in supernatural proportions. In Jesus' name.

Scriptures to Meditate On

• Genesis 24:21 NKJV *"And the man, wondering at her, remained silent so as to know whether the LORD had made his journey prosperous or not."*

• Exodus 8:27 NKJV *"We will go three days' journey into the wilderness and sacrifice to the LORD our God as He will command us."*

• Ezra 7:9 NKJV *"On the first day of the first month he began his journey from Babylon, and on the first day of the fifth month he came to Jerusalem, according to the good hand of his God upon him."*

• 1 Corinthians 16:6 NKJV *"And it may be that I will remain, or even spend the winter with you, that you may send me on my journey, wherever I go."*

Exercise

In this exercise I want you to look back at all the things that God has brought you through. Thank Him and bless the situation that you are going through presently. Speak and pray for someone that is going down a road that has been a huge mountain for him or her. Lay down your mountain for a moment and carry someone else's burden. Lay down your burden and place it on the altar. Allow the Lord to move through you to minister to one that is in need as well. You will find that often breakthrough comes when you sow into another's life that is in need. There is nothing more rewarding than seeing the face of pain turn into the face of joy. Try it. You'll like it!

Revelatory Understanding

(John Natale)

revelatory |ˈrevələˌtôrē, riˈvel-|
adjective
revealing something hitherto unknown: an invigorating and revelatory performance.

understanding |ˌəndərˈstandiNG|
noun
the ability to understand something; comprehension: foreign visitors with little understanding of English.
• the power of abstract thought; intellect: a child of sufficient intelligence and understanding.
• an individual's perception or judgment of a situation: my understanding was that he would try to find a new supplier.
• sympathetic awareness or tolerance: a problem that needs to be handled with understanding.
• an informal or unspoken agreement or arrangement: he and I have an understanding | he had only been allowed to come on the understanding that he would be on his best behavior.

One of the great stories that you can read in the Word is the life of Solomon. When he opens up his heart and cries out for help, he does not look to material things or blessing but he wanted divine revelation and wisdom. He showed his true character and passion for the deeper of things of God. We spend most of our time living in the realm of simplicity and comfort zone scenarios simply because the church (which is us) has become so complacent and deceived. When the Gifts are used and demonstrated with power, things happen, big things happen. One reason why the gifts do not flourish is because it causes people to be uncomfortable. Now the question is, are you comfortable or uncomfortable?

In this chapter of Revelation and Understanding, the Holy Spirit will give you everything you need. There is time to change, and there is time to renew. All things have become new! All things have become new! Say it again! I can feel the Holy Spirit as I write this to you. Now remember this all the days of your life and never forget. Nehemiah built a wall with limited resources and limited men. It was his determination and belief that all things are possible that allowed him to do this. I write this to you to encourage you and to challenge you. Revelation comes because the individual is willing to go farther and deeper. How much do you trust him? This manual is nothing but a tool to help you, but in the end, you will make the choice; you will fight the fight, and you will make the impact in your life and in the impossible. What these gifts are all about is to make the name of Jesus famous in your life and all those individuals that come across your path.

In 1 Corinthians 12:7-10, the spiritual gifts are brought to our attention. These include the four revelatory gifts: word of knowledge, word of wisdom, discerning of spirits and prophecy. Let's look at the word of knowledge, the word of wisdom and the discernment of spirits. They are known as the revelatory gifts because through divine revelation they allow the believer to see and to understand.

Word of Knowledge - Supernatural revelation as to a piece of knowledge, which would be naturally unknown to the recipient.

Word of Wisdom - Supernatural impartation of wisdom beyond the natural wisdom of the recipient.

Discerning of Spirits - A God-given ability to distinguish the spirit motivating a person or event.

Prophecy - To foretell or predict or to declare by or as if by divine inspiration.

We define them for clarity's sake but with all the things of God, there is a depth and a mystery about them that goes beyond mere human words and understanding. God is so good! God will use these revelatory gifts to accomplish many purposes: to lead people to Christ, to build up faith, to heal, and to expose the inner heart of the believer. They will allow you to speak and teach more effectively. As with all the gifts we need to be very careful that we do not focus on just one. There are many times in my life that I have come across people that actually have idolized a gift, especially the prophetic. We must not go beyond anything that the Lord is not saying or doing.

Words of Knowledge

We will expose in more detail the word of knowledge. It is supernatural revelation by the Holy Spirit. These scenarios can be about the past or the present. It is a word from the Lord that the recipient would have no other way of knowing. It is a word for a particular time or individual. It can be released individually or corporately. There is no class or college requirement to receive the word of knowledge. It is a gift operating purely in the Spirit.

Revelation is understanding, which is directly given as a gift from God to believers and includes an understanding of the scriptures by which only the Spirit of God can give. For this reason, our own thoughts and desires come from our human mind. Revelation is given by the mind of Christ. Biblical understanding can be a matter of reason, merely reading and understanding the text in your own interpretation, but revelation is understanding in a measure that is physically impossible with your own ability.

Words of Knowledge in Scriptures

• Mark 2:8 NKJV *"But immediately, when Jesus perceived in his spirit that they reasoned thus within themselves, He said to them, Why do you reason about these things in your hearts?."*

• Luke 1:41 NKJV *" And it happened, when Elizabeth heard the greeting of Mary, that the babe leaped in her womb; And Elizabeth was filled with the Holy Spirit"*

Words of knowledge are always received through the mind. The mind and thought processes can be used in many different ways. It can be through meditation and study of the scriptures, or God may address the mind through dreams and visions or perhaps through a clear word or thought. Many times I have been given words of knowledge through hearing the voice of God directly speak to me and tell me what's going on. There are times also when God will show you a scene of a person's life from the past. These are just a few examples how this gift works.

Word of Wisdom

Now we will look in more detail at the word of wisdom. Wisdom is the progression or forward movement of knowledge. It is a characteristic, which grows with experience. That experience carries victory and defeat. Wisdom needs to be sought when a word of knowledge is given or received because it includes the revelation of how to apply the God-given knowledge.

Operating in the Word of Wisdom

The word of wisdom is the icing on the cake to the word of knowledge. When we receive a word of knowledge, it is absolutely critical to seek the word of wisdom to know how to digest and to implement the ingredient in the individual's life. We need to discern if the word of knowledge was given to us for prayer purposes or if it was to be given to speak out and release.

You may receive it suddenly and you must be in tune with the Spirit of God to release the words that have been given timely and appropriately. It may come as a vision or dream or a natural scenario that plays out right in front of you. Jesus can do and use anything He wants to get the message across to you. Sometimes you just might get the information from an inner knowing and you receive words of wisdom for yourself or for others as you speak to them.

Word of Wisdom in the Scriptures

• 1 Kings 3:16-28 NKJV The story of Solomon and the two women who were disputing who's son had died. Solomon operated in wisdom to settle the dispute.

Discerning of Spirits

Now we will look deeper at the discerning of spirits. This gift is a God-given ability to discern which spirit is influencing a person. During critical times you must discern properly. You must be able to distinguish in the Spirit what is Godly and what is not-Operating in the Spirit of God and being sensitive in this area will allow you to successfully discern appropriately.

Discerning of spirits is not based on what we hear or see but more on what we are hearing the Holy Spirit say to you at that time. It is through revelation by the Holy Spirit. We can often know what a person is thinking or feeling just by looking at facial expressions or body language. Many times during the course of my travels, discernment was given the moment I landed at my destination or when I entered the church or home. Be sensitive to and aware of your surroundings at all times.

Always be cautious when operating in this gift. We are at a very pivotal and sensitive time in history both physically and spiritually. Never be quick to judge or critique something that looks a little different or doesn't seem to meet your standards. We need the gift of discernment more than ever before. Many lives are banking on it!

Scriptures of The Gift of Discernment

• Luke 4:34 NKJV *"Saying, Let us alone! What have we to do with you, Jesus of Nazareth? Did you come to destroy us? I know who You are, the Holy One of God."*

• Matthew 17:18 NKJV *"And Jesus rebuked the demon and it came out of him; and the child was cured from that very hour."*

Questions

1. Have you ever desired these gifts before? If not, why?

_____

_____

_____

_____

2. Do you believe that the gifts are an essential part of successful evangelism?

_____

_____

_____

_____

3. What is your belief system regarding the Gifts of the Spirit?

_____

_____

_____

_____

Prayer of Impartation

Lord I ask you to release the Gifts of the Spirit to me. Release the breakthrough of revelation and understanding, allow the impartation of these gifts to fill me as I desire them and equip me with all necessary tools to fulfill the Great Commission. Fill me with the fire of the Holy Spirit, in Jesus name I pray.

Scriptures to Meditate On

• Proverbs 29:18 NKJV *"Where there is no revelation, the people cast off restraint; But happy is he who keeps the law."*

• Luke 2:32 NKJV *"A light to bring revelation to the Gentiles, And the glory of Your people Israel."*

• Romans 16:25 NKVJ *"Now to Him who is able to establish you according to my gospel and the preaching of Jesus Christ, according to the revelation of the mystery kept secret since the world began"*

• Galatians 1:12 NKJV *"For I neither received it from man, nor was I taught it, but it came through the revelation of Jesus Christ."*

Exercise

After you have prayed this prayer and received all that the Lord has given you, pray in tongues and wait on the Holy Spirit to speak to you Be sensitive to the Holy Spirit and act on His leading. Call a friend or take some time to visit with someone you know needs prayer. As you begin to pray, open up your heart and spirit and allow to Lord to release the gifts to you and act as you are hearing Him speak. You will find that the gifts will flow very easily and in that place of prayer, you have just taken it to the next level—the fire and glory level!

The Fear of the Lord

(Adam LiVecchi)

fear |fi(ə)r|

noun

an unpleasant emotion caused by the belief that someone or something is dangerous, likely to cause pain, or a threat: drivers are threatening to quit their jobs in fear
after a cabby's murder | fear of increasing unemployment | he is prey to irrational
fears.
• archaic a mixed feeling of dread and reverence: the love and fear of God.
• (fear for) a feeling of anxiety concerning the outcome of something or the safety
and well-being of someone: police launched a search for the family amid fears for
their safety.
• the likelihood of something unwelcome happening: she could observe the other
guests without too much fear of attracting attention.

verb [with obj.]

be afraid of (someone or something) as likely to be dangerous, painful, or threaten-
ing: he said he didn't care about life so why should he fear death? | [with clause] :
farmers fear that they will lose business.
• [no obj.] (fear for) feel anxiety or apprehension on behalf of: I fear for the city
with this madman let loose in it.
• [with infinitive] avoid or put off doing something because one is afraid: they aim
to make war so horrific that potential aggressors will fear to resort to it.
• archaic regard (God) with reverence and awe.

"Everyone in the Kingdom fears the King." – Adam LiVecchi

In the Kingdom of God, there are many things that everyone has in common
even in spite of how different genuine believers can be. Everyone in the Kingdom
fears the King. Unfortunately not everyone in the "church" fears the Lord. Often
what we call the church, Jesus called backslidden. Let's put it this way, "If the gates

of hell are prevailing, it's not the church." When people don't fear the Lord it means there is unbelief, meaning they don't believe that God is who he says he is and they don't really believe that he will do what he said he would do in his word. Where the fear of the Lord is lacking often the knowledge of God is absent. Where the fear of the Lord is present there will be a strong emphasis on the obedience of faith. In the New Testament, one of the functions or manifestations of an apostle is to cause people to become obedient to faith by leading by example, see Romans 16:25-26. The prophetic movement should be marked by the fear of the Lord and the knowledge of God. The fear of the Lord and the knowledge of God go together like rice and beans, or like coffee and cream.

"My son, if thou wilt receive my words, and hide my commandments with thee; So that thou incline thine ear unto wisdom, and apply thine heart to understanding; Yea, if thou criest after knowledge, and liftest up thy voice for understanding; If thou seekest her as silver, and searchest for her as for hid treasures; Then shalt thou understand the fear of the LORD, and find the knowledge of God." Proverbs 2:1-5

To find the knowledge of God first the fear of the Lord must be understood. Unfortunately, one of the most elementary truths of Christianity has been lost. We must return to the fear of the Lord. When a people or a nation does not fear God, there is no moral restraint. When Abraham said his wife Sarah was his sister in Egypt, it was because he perceived the people didn't fear God.

"And Abraham said, Because I thought, Surely the fear of God is not in this place; and they will slay me for my wife's sake." Genesis 20:11

God gave King Abimelech a dream and the heathen King gave Abraham his wife back with out touching her. The fear of the Lord causes heathens to obey God; it's time we the church obey the voice of God. When the fear of the Lord is lost, we can no longer love God the way he desires to be loved. If the fear of God is absent, lawlessness will be present and evident, especially in the judicial system of that land that is lacking the fear of God. People start to call evil good and good evil. We see this all over the earth today. Lawlessness is when the laws of man directly oppose the laws of God. A few examples would be gay marriage, abortion or prostitution. The benefits of the fear of the Lord are both temporal and eternal.

"The fear of the LORD is the beginning of wisdom: a good understanding have all they that do his commandments: his praise endureth forever." (Psalm 111:10)

The fear of the Lord is the beginning of wisdom; wisdom is what should guide our decisions. When we obey God, we gain understanding. Discernment is for those who do the will of God. It's not enough to pray, "thy will be done." We must do the will of the Father. Jesus said, "My mother and brother are those who do the will of my father." If that verse doesn't bring the fear of the Lord upon you check and see if you have a pulse. There is a great sobriety that is going to come upon the sincere in the days to come. Part of honoring God is expressed by fearing him. When we say that we honor God, we are saying that we recognize who he really is. If we truly recognize who Jesus is we will love him and fear him enough to obey him.

In the Kingdom of God, the Holy Spirit teaches us all things and reminds us of all that Jesus has said. The Holy Spirit speaks what he hears from Jesus to us. The Word of God is the Holy Spirit's curriculum. The Kingdom of God cannot truly be understood without a comprehensive understanding of the fear of the Lord. To me it's alarming to hear about the Kingdom of God but hardly anything about the fear of the Lord. Alarms wake people up. Perhaps it's time we wake up! When the alarm sounds, we are then given a choice to either keep sleeping or wake up. I find it interesting how people can talk about the Kingdom of God but won't talk about the judgments of God.

"Come, ye children, hearken unto me: I will teach you the fear of the LORD."
(Psalm 34:11)

The fear of the Lord can be taught, but we must choose to learn. Taking the position of a learner means we must humble ourselves in the sight of God. Humility is both painful and beautiful. It's painful to the flesh, but it's beautiful to the Lord. When we truly fear the Lord we walk in humility towards people. Humility is not passivity, but that is another message for another day. Later in this chapter we will look into the New Testament and see how the fear of God should affect how we treat each other.

"For that they hated knowledge, and did not choose the fear of the LORD."
(Proverbs 1:29)

Clearly we see that the fear of the Lord is a choice. We must choose to fear the Lord and in doing so we enter into wisdom, which causes us to obey God. In the ground of obedience, understanding grows and true intimacy with the Lord Jesus is experienced and established. Through continual intimacy and fellowship with Jesus we come to really know him experientially. The truth that frees people is the truth that is known by experience. You can know the truth but that doesn't mean you will be set free. However, it's experiencing the truth that sets a person free.

"And why call ye me, Lord, Lord, and do not the things which I say?" (Luke 6:46)

Calling Jesus Lord doesn't mean he is our Lord but obeying Jesus is what really makes him our Lord. This person had sound doctrine; he understood the truth that Jesus was Lord but it just wasn't true to him because he did not do what Jesus said. The fear of the Lord brings this revelation to our attention before it's too late.

The fear of the Lord should affect every area of our lives. It begins with an inward reality. Then it is expressed in how we speak and live. Biblically speaking both loving God and fearing God directly affect how we treat each other and what we teach our children. Here are the two illustrations of this truth from the book of Deuteronomy. Often loving God is expressed by doing something and fearing God is expressed by not doing something. At other times our love for God and fear of him just simply causes us to obey him.

Loving God – Deuteronomy 6:4-7 *"Hear, O Israel: The LORD our God is one LORD: And thou shalt love the LORD thy God with all thine heart, and with all thy soul, and with all thy might. And these words, which I command thee this day, shall be in thine heart: And thou shalt teach them diligently unto thy children, and shalt talk of them when thou sittest in thine house, and when thou walkest by the way, and when thou liest down, and when thou risest up."*

Fearing God – Deuteronomy 6:1-2 *"Now these are the commandments, the statutes, and the judgments, which the LORD your God commanded to teach you, that ye might* *do them in the land whither ye go to possess it: That thou mightest fear the LORD thy God, to keep all his statutes and his commandments, which I command thee, thou, and thy son, and thy son's son, all the days of thy life; and that thy days may be prolonged."*

Our children and the poor of our community know how much we really fear and love God. The fear of the Lord affects how we treat those who Jesus called the "Least of these."

"And now, Israel, what doth the LORD thy God require of thee, but to fear the LORD thy God, to walk in all his ways, and to love him, and to serve the LORD thy God with all thy heart and with all thy soul, To keep the commandments of the LORD, and his statutes, which I command thee this day for thy good? Behold, the heaven and the heaven of heavens is the LORD'S thy God, the earth also, with all that therein is. Only the LORD had a delight in thy fathers to love them, and he chose their seed after them, even you above all people, as it is this day. Circumcise therefore the foreskin of your heart, and be no more stiffnecked. For the LORD your God is God of gods, and Lord of lords, a great God, a mighty, and a terrible, which regardeth not persons, nor taketh reward: He doth execute the judgment of the fatherless and widow, and loveth the stranger, in giving him food and raiment. Love ye therefore the stranger: for ye were strangers in the land of Egypt. Thou shalt fear the LORD thy God; him shalt thou serve, and to him shalt thou cleave, and swear by his name."(Deuteronomy 10:12-20)

The way we live shows what we really believe to be true. Our lifestyle clearly shows our value system and priorities. The question is are they based on Kingdom or tradition? Do we have Jesus or religion? Do we care for people or only for ourselves?

During the Protestant Reformation, the doctrine of the priesthood or the priesthood of the believers was reinstituted. In our day that doctrine is coming into manifestation in our lives. The Protestant Reformation was about reforming the doctrine; the reformation that is upon us now is about reforming our lifestyle. The fear of the Lord caused Martin Luther not to fear the Catholic Church, so he pounded the 95 theses to the door in Wittenberg, Germany. The same Spirit of the Fear of the Lord is going to cause us to begin to live out what Jesus taught and commanded at all costs. Now we don't have 95 theses, but we understand the truth. That truth has been historically proven and now it's time to be lived out. In a time where sound doctrine will not endure, God will raise up voices in the wilderness to declare the full counsel of God. The truth of God's word will begin to burn in the hearts of men and women again. The prophetic and the apostolic will work together being built directly upon Jesus Christ who is their Chief Cornerstone. When we fear God, Jesus is all we will build on. When we fear the Lord, we remember where he has taken us from, but we must not lose sight of where he is taking us.

"Looking unto Jesus the author and finisher of our faith; who for the joy that was set before him endured the cross, despising the shame, and is set down at the right hand of the throne of God." (Hebrews 12:2)

We are supposed to run looking unto Jesus because as we look at him and follow him we become like him. To simplify it, the fear of the Lord causes us to live like Christ. God has a higher standard than the law; it's his Son Jesus who fulfilled the law. Here is a paraphrased quote of Dietrich Bonheoffer from the book The Cost of Discipleship, "that under the law there was only a penalty for doing what is wrong, but following Jesus under grace means we suffer for doing good." Jesus is the standard and it's time we remember that once again and live like we believe it.

"So shall they fear the name of the LORD from the west, and his glory from the rising of the sun. When the enemy shall come in like a flood, the Spirit of the LORD shall lift up a standard against him. And the Redeemer shall come to Zion, and unto them that turn from transgression in Jacob, saith the LORD." (Isaiah 59:19-20)

The standard that the Spirit of the Lord raises up is Jesus. The west fearing the Lord is essential if western civilization is going to continue to exist in a civilized way. Moral decay can manifest through outward anarchy and civil unrest. Our economy decaying is merely an outward manifestation of our moral decay. If we repent now, then the fear of the Lord will return to the church and God's glory will rise as Jesus becomes the standard. I personally want to see the world change, but it will not happen until the church wakes up. Our repentance is essential if anything God is going to do in our day is going to be sustainable. Repent, means to change the way one thinks. If we change the way we think, then we will change the way we live; then the world will change. Perhaps the fear of the Lord will cause a real change of heart and a real change of mind in our day. I believe this is inevitable and will happen. The question is do we say yes to the voice of God? Or will it be another generation that receives the blessing that God has desired for us to have? This happened to Israel and Moses. They died overlooking the place God said was theirs. The will of God is heard. The question is do we have ears to hear what the Spirit of the Lord is saying? In the book of Revelation we see Isaiah 59:19 in action. Jesus brought strong rebukes to the churches in Asia. He ended his discourse each time with, "he that has ears to hear let him hear what the Spirit is saying to the church." Hear the Spirit of the Lord was raising the standard. Jesus declared the standard and he was trusting that the Holy Spirit would bring application to his word to each person and to the church in Asia as a whole. In the fear of the Lord there is radical trust for God. If Jesus is the standard, then we truly do fear the Lord. True fascination of the Lord starts by having reverence for the Lord.

When the prophetic is rooted in the fear of the Lord, it will be humble and accountable. Ephesians 5:21 says, *"Submitting yourselves one to another in the fear of God."* Fearing God means we submit to one another. To some people that is even uncomfortable to read, let alone do.

"For ye may all prophesy one by one, that all may learn, and all may be comforted. And the spirits of the prophets are subject to the prophets." (1 Corinthians 14:31-32)

The Spirit of the Prophet being subject to the Prophets is a great demonstration of submitting to one another in the fear of God. Paul the Apostle under the influence of the Holy Spirit gives deep insight and also practical application.

Fearing God means we don't apologize for who he really is or what he says and values and wills. Jesus doesn't need a defendant; he doesn't need to be sold. He needs to be obeyed and demonstrated. As we obey his word, his love, power and grace is displayed to others. What's interesting is when people see what Jesus is really like they actually want him. He is called the Desire of the Nations for a reason. The fear of the Lord releases urgency for obedience that is needed in the church like never before. Again the fear of the Lord that is clean and enduring forever causes us to run to the Lord not from him.

Questions

1. Do you fear the Lord in a healthy way?

_____

_____

_____

_____

2. Does the Fear of the Lord cause you to run to the Lord or away from him?

_____

_____

_____

_____

3. Have you thought of fear God as a negative thing?

_____

_____

_____

_____

Prayer of Impartation

Father teach me to fear you just as Jesus did. Let all my meditations, ambitions, desires, words and actions be pleasing in your sight. Help me to choose the fear of the Lord and find the knowledge of God.

Scriptures to Meditate On

• Psalm 25:14 *"The secret of the LORD is with them that fear him; and he will show them his covenant."*

• Psalm 27:1 *"The LORD is my light and my salvation; whom shall I fear? the LORD is the strength of my life; of whom shall I be afraid?"*

• Psalm 34:11 *"Come, ye children, hearken unto me: I will teach you the fear of the LORD."*

Exercise

Read the verses below and examine yourself. Take communion at home. Take a while to confess and allow the fear of the Lord to come upon you. Ask the Lord to cleanse you from secret faults, see Psalm 19:12.

1 Corinthians 11:23-32 *"For I have received of the Lord that which also I delivered unto you, That the Lord Jesus the same night in which he was betrayed took bread: And when he had given thanks, he brake it, and said, Take, eat: this is my body, which is broken for you: this do in remembrance of me. After the same manner also he took the cup, when he had supped, saying, This cup is the new testament in my blood: this do ye, as oft as ye drink it, in remembrance of me. For as often as ye eat this bread, and drink this cup, ye do show the Lord's death till he come. Wherefore whosoever shall eat this bread, and drink this cup of the Lord, unworthily, shall be guilty of the body and blood of the Lord. But let a man examine himself, and so let him eat of that bread, and drink of that cup. For he that eateth and drinketh unworthily, eateth and drinketh damnation to himself, not discerning the Lord's body. For this cause many are weak and sickly among you, and many sleep. For if we would judge ourselves, we should not be judged. But when we are judged, we are chastened of the Lord, that we should not be condemned with the world."*

Discernment

(Adam LiVecchi)

In researching and studying discernment and the gift of discerning of spirits I stumbled upon a writing of Jonathan Edwards on the topic. It was so good; we made it a mandatory reading for the prophetic school and we decided to put it in this manual. I consider this to be one of the very best if not the best writing on discernment I have ever read. The fruit in Jonathan Edwards' life is undeniably good and long lasting. He was called "America's greatest theologian." What I love about this man of God is he was a revivalist and a theologian. He was full of passion and knowledge. These are the kinds of people that we need in this hour. God is raising up men and women of honor and courage, who will stand in the very counsel of God and boldly declare his word. Another reason this writing was included in this manual is because from this writing you can get an un-biased opinion on the topic of discernment and apply it to today. Opposed to a supposed "discernment ministry," which slams everyone who doesn't think look like them or do things their way. Often in discernment we discern everyone else's issues but not our own. Jesus called that hypocrisy. Discernment must first be applied to ourselves then the rest of the world.

Jonathan Edwards's Theology of Discernment
(This material is condensed and adapted from
The Distinguishing Marks of a Work of the Spirit of God.)

"Beloved, do not believe every spirit, but test the spirits to see whether they are from God; because many false prophets have gone out into the world." (1 John 4:1)

In the apostolic age there was the greatest outpouring of the Spirit of God that ever was. But as the influences of the true Spirit abounded, counterfeits also abounded. The devil was abundant in mimicking both the ordinary and extraordinary influences of the Spirit of God. This made it very necessary that the church of Christ should be furnished with some certain rules—distinguishing and clear marks—by which she might proceed safely in judging of the true from the false. The giving of such rules is the plain design of 1 John 4, where this matter is more expressly and fully treated than anywhere else in the Bible. In this extraordinary day, when there is so much talk about the work of the Spirit, we must carefully apply these principles. Before the apostle proceeds to lay down the signs, first, he exhorts Christians against an over-credulousness: *"Beloved, do not believe every spirit, but test the spirits to see whether they are from God."* And second, he shows that there are many counterfeits: "because many false prophets have gone out into the world." These false spirits pretend not only to have the Spirit of God and extraordinary gifts of inspiration, but also to be the great friends and favorites of heaven, to be eminently holy persons, and to have much of the ordinary saving, sanctifying influences of the Spirit of God on their hearts. Therefore we are to examine and try their pretenses.

My design therefore is to show what are the true, certain, and distinguishing evidences of a work of the Spirit of God. And here I would observe that we are to take the Scriptures as our guide. This is the great and standing rule, which God has given to His church, in order to guide them in things relating to the great concerns of their souls. Scripture is an infallible and sufficient rule. It undoubtedly contains sufficient precepts to guide the church in this great affair of discerning a true work of God. Without such principles, the church would lie open to woeful delusions and would be exposed without remedy to be imposed on and devoured by its enemies. I shall confine myself to the principles I find in 1 John 4. But before I proceed particularly to speak of these, I will prepare my way first by observing what are not reliable evidences whether something is a work of the Spirit of God.

INVALID ARGUMENTS

These things are no evidence that a work is or is not from the Spirit of God:

"We've Never Done It That Way Before"
Nothing can be concluded from the fact that a work is carried on in a very unusual and extraordinary way, provided it does not violate any biblical principles. "What the church is used to" is not a rule by which we are to judge. God often works in extraordinary ways.

The prophecies of Scripture give us reason to think that God has things to accomplish that have not yet been seen. The Holy Spirit is sovereign in His operation. We ought not to limit God where He has not limited Himself.

"People's Reactions Are Too Strong"

A work is not to be condemned merely because of any effects on men such as tears, trembling, groans, loud outcries, agonies of body, or the failing of bodily strength. The Scripture nowhere gives us any such rule. We cannot conclude that persons are under the influence of the Holy Spirit just because we see such effects upon their bodies (this is not given as a mark of the true Spirit). Nor on the other hand, should we conclude from such outward appearances that persons are not under the influence of the Spirit of God.

It does seem, however, that a proper sense of gospel truth should provoke a strong response—failing of strength, bodily agonies, and even loud outcries. Surely the misery of hell is so dreadful and eternity so vast that if a person gains a clear understanding of it, it would be more than his feeble frame could bear—especially if at the same time he saw himself in great danger of being eternally lost. If a person saw himself hanging over a great pit, full of fierce and glowing flames, by a thread that he knew to be very weak and not sufficient to bear his weight; if he knew that multitudes had been in such circumstances before and that most of them had fallen and perished; if he saw nothing within reach that he could take hold of to save him, what distress would he be in! How ready to think that now the thread was breaking—that now, this minute, he should be swallowed up in those dreadful flames! Wouldn't he naturally cry out in such circumstances?

No wonder that the wrath of God, even when manifested but a little to the soul, overwhelms human strength! After all, both Saul of Tarsus and the Philippian jailer trembled from real convictions of conscience.

"People Are Talking About It Too Much"

The fact that something provokes a great deal of noise about religion is no argument against its validity. Although true religion is never ostentatious like that of the Pharisees—yet human nature is such that it is morally impossible to experience renewal and revival without causing a commotion in the community.

Surely, there is no reason to dismiss a work of God's Spirit just because people are very much moved. After all, spiritual and eternal things are so great and of such infinite concern, that it would be absurd for people to be only moderately moved and affected by them. Remember, people said of the apostles that they had turned the world upside down (Acts 17:6).

"People Are Imagining Things"

It is no argument that something is not the work of the Spirit of God because people have great impressions made on their imaginations. Our nature is such that we cannot think of invisible things without a degree of imagination. The more engaged the mind and affections are, the more intense will be the imagination.

This is especially true when the truth being contemplated is new to the mind and takes hold of the emotions. When someone is struck with extreme dread, and when at conversion that sense of dread gives way immediately to extreme delight, it is no wonder if such a person cannot easily distinguish between that which is imaginary and that which is intellectual and spiritual. Many people are apt to lay too much weight on the imaginary part, and are most ready to speak of that when they testify of their experiences. In such cases God seems to condescend to their circumstances and deal with them as babes.

"People Just Do What They See Others Doing"

It is no sign that a work is not from the Spirit of God just because it spreads by means of example. We know that it is God's manner to use various means in carrying on His work. It is no argument against God's involvement in something that a particular means is used to accomplish it.

And certainly it is agreeable to Scripture that persons should be influenced by one another's good example. The Scripture directs us to set good examples to that end (Matt. 5:16; 1 Peter 3:1; 1 Tim. 4:12; Titus 2:7). It also directs us to be influenced by the good examples of others (2 Cor. 8:1–7; Phil. 3:17; 1 Cor. 4:16–17; 2 Thess. 3:9; 1 Thess. 1:7). It appears that example is one of God's means. It is both a scriptural and a reasonable way of carrying on God's work.

"People Are Getting Carried Away"

It is no sign that a work is not from the Spirit of God just because many are guilty of great imprudence's and irregularities in their conduct. God pours out His Spirit to make men holy, not to make them politicians. It is no wonder that in a mixed multitude of all sorts—wise and unwise, young and old, people with weak and strong natural abilities, and people under strong impressions of mind—many behave themselves imprudently. There are but few that know how to conduct themselves under vehement affections of any kind. A thousand imprudences will not prove a work to be not of the Spirit of God. Often things occur that are even contrary to the rules of God's holy Word. That it should be this way is due to the exceeding weakness of human nature, together with the remaining darkness and corruption of those who are yet under the saving influences of God's Spirit. The church at Corinth, with all the problems Paul had to correct, is a New Testament example of a true work of the Spirit, accompanied by many human imprudences.

Lukewarmness in religion is abominable. Zeal is an excellent grace. Yet above all other Christian virtues, this needs to be strictly watched and searched, for corruption—and particularly pride and human passion—is exceedingly prone to mix unobserved with zeal.

"People Are Deluded"

Errors in judgment, and even some delusions of Satan might be intermixed with a work; yet that does not mean that the work in general is not wrought by the Spirit of God.

We are not to expect that the Spirit of God should guide us infallibly as He did the apostles. Yet otherwise godly people fail to understand this. Many godly persons have undoubtedly in this and other ages exposed themselves to woeful delusions, by a tendency to lay too much weight on subjective impulses and impressions, as if they were immediate revelations from God to signify something future, or to direct them where to go and what to do.

"People Are Falling into Error"

If some supposed "converts" fall away into gross errors, or scandalous practices, it is no argument that the work in general is not the work of the Spirit of God. Counterfeits are no proof that a thing is untrue: such things are always expected in a time of reformation.

If we look into church history, we shall find that every great revival has been attended with many such things. Instances of this nature in the apostles' days were innumerable; some fell away into gross heresies, others into vile practices—even though they seemed to be the subjects of the Spirit's work and were even accepted for a while as true disciples.

One example of these was Judas, who was intimately conversant with the disciples. Yet he was not discovered or suspected until he discovered himself by his scandalous practice. Jesus Himself treated Judas as if he had truly been a disciple, even investing him with the character of apostle, sending him forth to preach the gospel, and enduing him with miraculous gifts of the Spirit. For although Christ knew him, yet He did not then clothe Himself with the character of omniscient Judge and searcher of hearts, but acted the part of a minister of the visible church and therefore rejected him not.

The devil's sowing of tares is no proof that a true work of the Spirit of God is not gloriously carried on.

"The Preachers Emphasize Judgment Too Much"

It is no argument that a work is not from the Spirit of God that it seems to be promoted by ministers insisting very much on the terrors of God's holy law. If hell's torments are real and multitudes are in great danger of falling into God's eternal condemnation or being lulled into insensitivity about it, then why is it not proper for pastors to take great pains to make people conscious of the awful truth? Why should people not be told as much of the truth as can be?

If I am in danger of going to hell, and if I am prone to neglect due care to avoid it, the greatest kindness anyone can do for me is to tell me the truth in the liveliest manner. We all would go to any extreme necessary to warn people of life-threatening temporal danger; why should we not do even more when it comes to eternal dangers?

Some talk of it as an unreasonable thing to frighten persons to heaven; but I think it is a reasonable thing to endeavor to frighten persons away from hell. They stand on its brink and are just ready to fall into it and are senseless of their danger. Is it not a reasonable thing to frighten a person out of a house on fire? Not that I think that only the law should be preached. The gospel is to be preached as well as the law. In fact, the law is to be preached only to make way for the gospel. The main work of ministers is to preach the gospel: "Christ is the end of the law for righteousness" (Rom. 10:4). A minister would miss it very much if he were to insist so much on the terrors of the law that he forgot his Lord and neglected to preach the Gospel. Still, the law is very much to be insisted on, and the preaching of the Gospel is likely to be in vain without it.

BIBLICAL SIGNS OF THE TRUE SPIRIT'S WORK

Having shown what are not sufficient evidences to conclude that the Spirit of God is not in a work, I now proceed as was proposed, to show positively what are the distinguishing biblical marks of a work of the Spirit of God. And in this, as I said before, I shall confine myself wholly to the evidences given us by the apostle in 1 John 4. Here this matter is particularly addressed more plainly and fully than anywhere else in the Bible. And in speaking to these marks, I shall take them in the order in which I find them in the chapter.

It Exalts the True Christ

"By this you know the Spirit of God: every spirit that confesses that Jesus Christ has come in the flesh is from God; and every spirit that does not confess Jesus is not from God." (I John 4:2–3a)

When a ministry raises people's esteem of the one true Jesus Christ, who was born of a virgin and was crucified—if it confirms and establishes their minds in the truth that He is the Son of God and the Savior of men—then it is a sure sign that it is from the Spirit of God.

If the spirit at work among a people convinces them of Christ and leads them to Him; if it confirms their minds in the belief of the history of Christ as He appeared in the flesh; if it teaches them that He is the Son of God, who was sent of God to save sinners; if it reveals that He is the only Savior, and that they stand in great need of Him; and if it begets in them higher and more honorable thoughts of Christ than they used to have; if it inclines their affections more to Him—that is a sure sign that it is the true and right Spirit. This is true even though we are ultimately incapable of determining whether anyone's conviction or affections reflect real saving faith.

The words of the apostle are remarkable. The person to whom the Spirit testifies must be that Jesus who appeared in the flesh—not another Christ in His stead. It cannot be some mystical, fantastical Christ, such as the "inner light" extolled by the Quakers. This imaginary Christ diminishes their esteem of and dependence on Jesus as He came in the flesh. The true Spirit of God gives testimony for that Jesus alone. The devil has a fierce hatred against Christ, especially in His office as the Savior of men. Satan mortally hates the story and doctrine of redemption; he never would go about to stress these truths. The Spirit that inclines men's hearts to the Seed of the woman is not the spirit of the serpent that has such an irreconcilable enmity against Him.

It Opposes Satan's Interests

"You are from God, little children, and have overcome them; because greater is He who is in you than he who is in the world. They are from the world; therefore they speak as from the world, and the world listens to them" (1 John 4: 4–5)

When the spirit that is at work operates against the interests of Satan's kingdom, against sin, and against worldly lusts—this is a sure sign that it is a true, and not a false spirit.

Here is a plain antithesis. The apostle is comparing those who are influenced by two opposite spirits, the true and the false. The difference is plain: the one is of God, and overcomes the spirit of the world; the other is of the world, and is obsessed with the things of the world. The devil is called, "he who is in the world."

What the apostle means by, "the world," or "the things that are in the world," we learn by his own words: "*Do not love the world, nor the things in the world. If anyone loves the world, the love of the Father is not in him. For all that is in the world, the lust of the flesh and the lust of the eyes and the boastful pride of life, is not from the Father, but is from the world (2:15–16).*" So by "the world" the apostle evidently means everything that pertains to the interest of sin. The term also comprehends all the corruptions and lusts of men, as well as all those acts and objects by which they are gratified.

We may also safely determine from what the apostle says that whatever lessens people's esteem of the pleasures, profits, and honors of the world; whatever turns their hearts from an eager pursuit after these things; whatever engages them in a due concern about eternity and causes them earnestly to seek the kingdom of God and His righteousness; whatever convinces them of the dreadfulness of sin, the guilt it brings, and the misery to which it exposes, must be the Spirit of God.

It is not to be supposed that Satan would convince men of sin or awaken the conscience. It can no way serve his end to make that candle of the Lord shine the brighter. It is for his interest, whatever he does, to lull conscience asleep and keep it quiet. To have that with its eyes and mouth open in the soul would tend to clog and hinder all his designs of darkness. The awakened conscience would evermore disturb his affairs, cross his interests, and disquiet him. Would the devil, when he is about to establish people in sin, take such a course? Would he make them more careful, inquisitive, and watchful to discern what is sinful, and to avoid future sins, and to be more wary of the devil's temptations?

The man who has an awakened conscience is the least likely to be deceived of any man in the world; it is the drowsy, insensible, stupid conscience that is most easily blinded. The Spirit that operates thus cannot be the spirit of the devil; Satan will not cast out Satan (Matt. 12:25–26). Therefore if we see persons made sensible of the dreadful nature of sin and the displeasure of God against it, we may conclude that whatever effects this concern is from the Spirit of God.

It Points People to the Scriptures

"We are from God; he who knows God listens to us; he who is not from God does not listen to us. By this we know the spirit of truth and the spirit of error (1 John 4: 6)." The spirit that causes people to have a greater regard for the Holy Scriptures and establishes them more in the truth and divinity of God's Word is certainly the Spirit of God.

The devil never would attempt to beget in persons a regard to the divine Word. A spirit of delusion will not incline persons to seek direction at the mouth of God. *"To the law and to the testimony! (Isa. 8:20)"* is never the cry of evil spirits who have no light in them. On the contrary, it is God's own direction to discover their delusions. Would the spirit of error, in order to deceive men, beget in them a high opinion of the infallible Word? Would the prince of darkness, in order to promote his kingdom of darkness, lead men to the sun? The devil has always shown a mortal spite and hatred towards that holy book, the Bible. He has done all in his power to extinguish that light, or else draw men off from it. He knows it to be that light by which his kingdom of darkness is to be overthrown. He has long experienced its power to defeat his purposes and baffle his designs. It is his constant plague. It is the sword of the Spirit that pierces him and conquers him. It is that sharp sword that we read of in Revelation 19:15, which proceeds out of the mouth of Him that sat on the horse, with which He smites His enemies. Every text is a dart to torment the old serpent. He has felt the stinging smart thousands of times.

Therefore the devil is engaged against the Bible and hates every word in it. We may be sure that he never will attempt to raise anyone's esteem of it.

It Elevates Truth

"We know the spirit of truth and the spirit of error (1 John 4:6)."

Another rule by which to judge spirits is that whatever operates as a spirit of truth, leading people to truth, convincing them of those things that are true—we may safely determine that it is a right and true spirit.

For instance, if the spirit at work makes men more aware than they used to be of the central gospel truths: that there is a God; that He is a great and a sin-hating

God; that life is short and very uncertain; that there is another world; that they have immortal souls; that they must give account of themselves to God; that they are exceeding sinful by nature and practice; that they are helpless in themselves—then that spirit operates as a spirit of truth. He represents things as they truly are. He brings men to the light.

On the other hand, the spirit of darkness will not uncover and make manifest the truth. Christ tells us that Satan is a liar, and the father of liars. His kingdom is a kingdom of darkness. It is upheld and promoted only by darkness and error. Satan has all his power and dominion by darkness. Whatever spirit removes our darkness and brings us to the light undeceives us. If I am brought to the truth and am made aware of things as they really are, my duty is immediately to thank God for it without inquiring by what means I have such a benefit.

It Results in Love for God and Others
"The one who does not love does not know God, for God is love (1 John 4:8)."

If the spirit that is at work among a people operates as a spirit of love to God and man, it is a sure sign that it is the Spirit of God. This last mark, which the apostle gives of the true Spirit, he seems to speak of as the most eminent. He devotes more space to it and so insists much more largely on it than all the rest.

When the spirit that is at work among the people brings many of them to high and exalting thoughts of the Divine Being and His glorious perfections; when it works in them an admiring, delightful sense of the Excellency of Jesus Christ, representing Him as the chief among ten thousand and altogether lovely; when it makes Him precious to the soul, winning and drawing the heart with those motives and incitements to free love of God and the wonderful dying love of Christ—it must be the Spirit of God.

"We love, because He first loved us," verse 19 says. The spirit that makes the soul long after God and Christ must be the Spirit of God. When we desire the presence and communion of the divine Savior, acquaintance with Him, conformity to Him, a life that pleases and honors Him, we must be under the influence of His Spirit.

Moreover, the spirit that quells contentions among men gives a spirit of peace and good-will, excites to acts of outward kindness, earnestly desires the salvation of souls, and arouses love for all the children of God and followers of Christ. I say that when a spirit operates after this manner, there is the highest kind of evidence that this is the Holy Spirit.

Indeed, there is a counterfeit love that often appears among those who are led by a spirit of delusion. There is commonly in the wildest enthusiasts a kind of union and affection arising from self-love. It is occasioned by their agreeing on issues where they greatly differ from all others and for which they are objects of ridicule from the rest of mankind. That naturally will cause them so much the more to prize those peculiarities that make them the objects of others' contempt. (Thus the ancient Gnostics and the wild fanatics that appeared at the beginning of the Reformation boasted of their great love to one another—one sect of them in particular calling themselves "the family of love.") But this is quite another thing than that Christian love I have just described.

There is enough said in this passage of the nature of a truly Christian love to distinguish it from all such counterfeits. It is love that arises from apprehension of the wonderful riches of the free grace and sovereignty of God's love to us in Jesus Christ. It is attended with a sense of our own utter unworthiness (see vv. 9–11, 19). The surest character of true, divine, supernatural love—distinguishing it from counterfeits that arise from a natural self-love—is that the Christian virtue of humility shines in it. It is a love, which above all others renounces, abases, and annihilates what we term self. Christian love is a humble love (1 Cor. 13:4–5).

When, therefore, we see a love attended with a sense of one's own littleness, vileness, weakness, and utter insufficiency; when it is united with self-diffidence, self-emptiness, self-renunciation, and poverty of spirit—those are the manifest tokens of the Spirit of God. He that thus dwells in love dwells in God, and God in him.

CONCLUSION

These marks that the apostle has given us are sufficient to stand-alone and support themselves. They plainly show the finger of God and are sufficient to out-weigh a thousand such little objections as many make from oddities, irregularities, errors in conduct, and the delusions and scandals of some professors.

But here some may object. After all, the apostle Paul says in 2 Corinthians 11:13–14, *"Such men are false apostles, deceitful workers, disguising themselves as apostles of Christ. And no wonder, for even Satan disguises himself as an angel of light."*

To which I answer that this can be no objection against the sufficiency of these marks to distinguish the true from the false spirit in those false apostles and prophets—even when the devil is transformed into an angel of light. After all, the very reason the apostle John gave these marks was so that we could test the spirits. Therefore try the spirits by these rules and you will be able to distinguish the true spirit from the false—even under such a crafty disguise.

Prophetic Lessons

This section will be short lessons that will help you move forward in Prophetic Ministry. Remembering and practicing what you have learned will bring acceleration to your life, family and ministry. A truly prophetic life is a life that remembers what God has both said and done. Remembering what God has done positions us to be apart of what he is doing.

"I have more understanding than all my teachers: for thy testimonies are my meditation." (Psalm 119:99)

Apostolic Understanding of the Prophetic Ministry

(Adam LiVecchi)

"For ye may all prophesy one by one, that all may learn, and all may be comforted."
(1 Corinthians 14:31)

Here Paul the Apostle desired all to learn to prophesy. Truly he carried the heart of the Father and was a real genuine Spiritual Father. When the church gathers, there should be an atmosphere for learning. Spiritual Fathers are facilitators of learning and growth unto maturity. When the leader of a church is secure in his position, there will be an atmosphere that is conducive to learning. When the leader of a church is insecure, the atmosphere will be very sterile and controlled and all the learning will be limited to what he or she says and does. It was an Apostle who desired all to learn to prophesy, not a Prophet. When Paul mentioned people learning to prophesy he meant it. In the process of learning, there will be mistakes. The real issue is not about being wrong. It is ok to be wrong; however, it's not ok to stay wrong. In a church people must remain teachable or the prophetic will be contaminated in an almost unredeemable manner. Being teachable is one of the keys to learning. Apostles are the best facilitators of prophetic ministry because they understand its role in the big picture of God's plan. To have an understanding of true New Testament prophetic ministry, we must clearly understand the apostolic mission that Jesus entrusted the Apostles with. My Spiritual Father, Steve Stewart says it like this, "The church doesn't have a mission; the mission has a church." The mission or the Great Commission gives a context for New Testament prophetic ministry.

There is a difference between Old Testament and New Testament prophetic ministry but it's often not what people make it to be. You will hear well-known and well-respected Prophets say, "God is not judging people today." That is false! If God were not judging people today, then we would not need to preach the gospel. People are perishing, and we need to preach the gospel. Sometimes people will make it seem like God was in a bad mood in the Old Testament and all of a sudden in the

New Testament he was in a good mood. That is a lie because of a misunderstanding. When people try to explain what they don't understand, it releases confusion. Confusion is a breeding ground for division and deception. In the Old Testament, a vast majority of Prophetic ministry was calling people back to God. In the New Testament prophetic ministry is mainly about bringing God to people by the leading of the Holy Spirit and building up the people of God. There are times in the New Testament where God releases judgment or calls people back to himself but those are not as much of the norms as they were in the Old Testament. I will list a few of the New Testament prophetic experiences to Biblically qualify what was just stated.

Prophetic Experiences Related to the Proclamation of the Gospel and the Advancement of the Kingdom

• Acts 7 – Stephen sees Jesus standing at the right hand of God while he is preaching and being stoned. This encounter with the Lord was in the context of preaching the gospel and being persecuted. God released grace in the time of need and Stephen saw Jesus standing at the right hand of God.

• Acts 8 – Philip is translated after preaching the gospel to a Eunuch from Ethiopia.

• Acts 9 – Saul sees Jesus and becomes Paul. He is changed and blinded. God gives Ananias a detailed word of Knowledge where Saul was. Ananias prays for Saul and he receives his sight and gets filled with the Holy Spirit.

• Acts 10 – Cornelius' encounter with an Angel and Peter's trance were both about the Gospel going to Gentiles and Peter's diet change so he could have fellowship with Gentiles that God himself was desiring fellowship with. At the end of Acts 10, the Holy Spirit falls on 3,000 people while Peter is preaching the gospel. When the Gospel is preached, the Supernatural is released and the impossible becomes possible.

• Acts 12 – The Angel of the Lord releases Peter from Prison. He was imprisoned because of Jesus and was let out so that he could continue to preach the gospel. Later in the chapter the Angel of the Lord executes Herod after his political speech, where he failed to give glory to God for his oratory gift. He had killed James earlier for the gospel. The gospel was not going to be stopped, so the Lord executed Herod in front of a crowd and worms ate him. For those of you who don't believe in capital punishment, the Angel of the Lord does.

• Acts 13 – The Holy Spirit says, *"Separate Barnabas and Saul for the work I have called them to."* That work was to preach the gospel.

• Acts 16 – The Holy Spirit forbids Paul to go to Asia to preach. That same night he has a vision and understands it to be the Lord directing him to preach the gospel in Macedonia.

To simplify, the Apostolic ministry has been entrusted with the Advancement of the Kingdom through the proclamation of the gospel. The prophetic ministry fits and operates properly in the context of the great commission. When the prophetic functions in that manner, it bears fruit and usually remains pure. The New Testament prophetic ministry is primarily about the revelation of Jesus Christ and the advancement of the Kingdom through the preaching of the gospel. There are times where judgments are pronounced and the people of God are called back to the Lord. However the prophetic ministry is supposed to be more offensive in seeking to reach people and edifying the church to do so. Perhaps reaching people is edifying or building up the church? Instead of trying to predict or pronounce judgment on people because we haven't effectively reached out to them. We should simply reach them. Our job is not to merely prophesy about a revival. A revival is not what is needed, because nothing in the Kingdom is dead. We simply need to align ourselves with the King. Our job is to listen to him and declare what he is saying, that is prophetic ministry. Psalm 2:7 says, *"I will declare the decree: the LORD hath said unto me, Thou art my Son; this day have I begotten thee."*

The Spirit of Prophecy is the testimony of Jesus and it is given or released to produce worship unto God. Remember the gift of Prophecy is made available through the Spirit of Prophecy. It's a person who gives spiritual gifts because he is the Holy Spirit. In the two passages below we can see the gift of Prophecy and the Spirit of Prophecy both producing worship unto God. Prophecy is the "I told you so of God." Authentic prophecy produces real worship because it reveals the eternity of God; it reveals that before it happened he knew it would because he knows everything. Prophecy is about revealing the nature of God as an amazing Father who knows best. The prophetic demystified is God knows everything. He loves you and knows what's best so just do what he says. The real results people are looking for in life only come through obedience to the word.

The Gift of Prophecy and the Spirit of Prophecy

• Corinthians 14:24-25 *"But if all prophesy, and there come in one that believeth not, or one unlearned, he is convinced of all, he is judged of all: And thus are the secrets of his heart made manifest; and so falling down on his face he will worship God, and report that God is in you of a truth."*

• Revelation 19:10-15 *"And I fell at his feet to worship him. And he said unto me, See thou do it not: I am thy fellowservant, and of thy brethren that have the testimony of Jesus: worship God: for the testimony of Jesus is the spirit of prophecy. And I saw heaven opened, and behold a white horse; and he that sat upon him was called Faithful and True, and in righteousness he doth judge and make war. His eyes were as a flame of fire, and on his head were many crowns; and he had a name written, that no man knew, but he himself. And he was clothed with a vesture dipped in blood: and his name is called The Word of God. And the armies which were in heaven followed him upon white horses, clothed in fine linen, white and clean. And out of his mouth goeth a sharp sword, that with it he should smite the nations: and he shall rule them with a rod of iron: and he treadeth the winepress of the fierceness and wrath of Almighty God."*

3 Lessons to Never Forget

1. The Prophetic ministry is about advancing the Kingdom, not about building our own reputation or empire.

2. Both the Spirit of Prophecy and the Gift of prophecy are to produce unadulterated worship to God, in the person of Jesus Christ. The result of an open heaven and an open heart is worship to God.

3. Prophecy is to reveal the Supremacy of Jesus Christ and to identify that God is truly in the midst of his people and there is manifested proof to the outside world.

Notes

Displaying Prophetic Movement

(John Natale)

"Then Samuel took the horn of oil and anointed him in the midst of his brothers; and the Spirit of the LORD came upon David from that day forward. So Samuel arose and went to Ramah." (1 Samuel 16:13 NKJV)

Prophetic movement comes from individuals who are willing to risk and take measures into their own hands. Here we see David getting anointed by the prophet Samuel. The Lord made a choice to have someone anointed that would have been everyone's last choice to be king. This was the initiating factor to one man's ultimate destiny of kingship. David was a fierce warrior who did not fear opposition or anything that stood in his way. This lesson is about the choices you make and how they affect your life and everyone around you. Now let's look at

"David said to Saul, Let no man's heart fail because of this Philistine; your servant will go out and fight with him." (1 Samuel 17:31 NKJV)

Here we see a young teenager speaking with the confidence and determination of a seasoned veteran. How does David come up with this kind of courage and fearlessness behavior? Remember, as he was anointed there is a transfer of blessing and authority. David had no idea what his destiny was going to involve but his inner-man was crying out for justice and reformation. He now comes to he greatest roadblock of his life. Goliath. Here is where the rubber meets the road. Many times in your life you will experience scenarios that will test your prophetic promise. It is intentionally targeted to hinder your prophetic movement. Goliath was that test. David mentions to king Saul that he has killed the lion and also killed the bear. David was given supernatural strength and authority to defeat the animals that came his way but they were in no part hindrances to his forward advancement. The ground that David is about to walk on is the proving ground that ultimately carves out the foundation of his character and destination of prophetic promise.

"Then David said to the Philistine, You come to me with a sword, with a spear, and with a javelin. But I come to you in the name of the LORD of hosts, the God of the armies of Israel, whom you have defied." (1 Samuel 17:45 NKJV)

What an amazing display of confidence and boldness. He knows who he is and he knows the ramifications of what happens if he does not keep going in the direction he is going. This scene is a perfect example of a person that has vision, goals and a passion for success. Not just in the natural, but the spiritual. The greatest lesson we learn in this story is David's forward movement. Each step he took brought him closer to the fence that blocked his path and ultimately his fellow man. But as we see in the text, he prophesied to his situation. He called those things that are not as though they were. One scripture that can be applied here is this, *"Now faith is the substance of things hoped for, the evidence of things not seen."* Hebrews 11:1 NKJV

When Goliath came toward David, it says that David ran quickly toward the Philistine. We know the end of the story from here. The slingshot whips the stone out and it sinks into the head of the giant. Did David have the ability to make that shot with his own ability? Most likely not, but with help from the Lord, all things are possible. His victory over the giant was the initiating fuel touch point to his award –winning career if you would put it in today's English. This lesson was to show and teach you that during the course of your destiny and journey through life, there will be instrumental moments that define you and shape you. All the prophecies you have received and will receive will be tested and proven. But the journey is yours. You will have to show character and courage, strength and boldness. It does not come without a price and it always involves other people, ones that you embrace and others that you reject. But in the end, if you are faithful to the promise and tender to the tug, you will find yourself standing with your hand lifted high! Be sensitive in all things, stay focused and be encouraged! The best days of your life are ahead of you, not behind you!

3 Lessons to Never Forget

1. Destiny involves you and someone else around you.

2. Prophecy does not come to pass unless you act.

3. Prophetic words over your life are meant to cause natural movement that initiate spiritual advancement.

Notes

_____

_____

_____

_____

_____

_____

_____

_____

_____

_____

_____

_____

Encouraging Yourself in the Lord

(Adam LiVecchi)

"And it came to pass, when David and his men were come to Ziklag on the third day, that the Amalekites had invaded the south, and Ziklag, and smitten Ziklag, and burned it with fire; And had taken the women captives, that were therein: they slew not any, either great or small, but carried them away, and went on their way. So David and his men came to the city, and, behold, it was burned with fire; and their wives, and their sons, and their daughters, were taken captives. Then David and the people that were with him lifted up their voice and wept, until they had no more power to weep. And David's two wives were taken captives, Ahinoam the Jezreelitess, and Abigail the wife of Nabal the Carmelite. And David was greatly distressed; for the people spake of stoning him, because the soul of all the people was grieved, every man for his sons and for his daughters: but David encouraged himself in the LORD his God. And David said to Abiathar the priest, Ahimelech's son, I pray thee, bring me hither the ephod. And Abiathar brought thither the ephod to David. And David enquired at the LORD, saying, Shall I pursue after this troop? shall I overtake them? And he answered him, Pursue: for thou shalt surely overtake them, and without fail recover all." (1 Samuel 30:1-8)

The reason Ziklag was burned and the women and children were missing is because Saul did not execute the vengeance of God on the Amalekites as God desired him to, see 1 Samuel 28:18. Here David had to fight a battle that Saul was called to win. The first thing we need to know is what one generation doesn't do another generation will have to do. Before these scriptures David was rejected or sent home by the Philistines. You know it's a bad day when the devil doesn't even want you on his team. David suffered rejection for no apparent reason. Prophetic people must learn how to respond properly to rejection. Responding properly to rejection is one of the doorways to destiny. Here David has been on the run for over 10 years. His enemies reject him, his two wives are gone, his city is burned with fire and his friends want to stone him. With friends like that who needs enemies? Anyway his reaction to all this is what opened the door of the palace to him. The Word of the Lord tested him and he was found faithful.

After all the madness David went through he did one thing. He enquired of the Lord. The way he encouraged himself in the Lord was by positioning himself to hear from God. He didn't ask the Priest (or his pastor) to ask God, he asked the Lord himself and responded properly. Remember if we ask we shall receive. There are times when we will have to seek and knock, but nevertheless we will receive. Those who are hungry and thirsty for righteousness shall be filled. David asked the Lord two specific questions, (my paraphrase) 1. Should I fight? 2. Will I win? As soon as he got his answer immediately he pursued the enemy and recovered all just as God said he would. The most important part of our walk with God is our ability to listen to him and obey. If I said that a million times it would not be enough. David didn't ask vague questions, he asked specific questions and God gave him specific answers. David behaved like a King before he had a throne. That is the kind of faithfulness God is looking for. Don't wait for a title to do what God called you to do, just go for it.

3 Lessons to Never Forget

1. The next generation will have to fight the battles we don't fight. We must not allow our victory to be someone else's because we don't want to fight.

2. Responding properly to pressure prepares us for our destiny.

3. Positioning ourselves to hear God's voice is how we strengthen our self in the Lord.

Notes

Creating a Prophetic Atmosphere

(Adam LiVecchi)

"Rejoice evermore. Pray without ceasing. In every thing give thanks: for this is the will of God in Christ Jesus concerning you. Quench not the Spirit. Despise not prophesyings. Prove all things; hold fast that which is good." (1 Thessalonians 5:16-21)

Here the Apostle Paul boldly declares the will of God to the Thessalonians. He begins with rejoice always. We would not be able to rejoice always if God was not always in a good mood. God is in a good mood; we need to approach life with this understanding. Paul the Apostle gets the concept of praying always or without ceasing from the Gospel of Luke.

"And he spoke a parable unto them to this end, that men ought always to pray, and not to faint." (Luke 18:1)

The he is Jesus. The New Testament doesn't tell us to build a house of prayer it tells us to become one. Prayer is not primarily about our needs, but it is primarily about God's will. The most important part of prayer is not what we can say to God, but what God will say to us. Praying without ceasing is not just about night and day prayer; it's primarily about a posture of attentiveness to the Lord Jesus. His joy empowers us to rejoice and stay attentive to him. Prayer is about a two-way conversation. The first time God spoke to you and you heard his voice he actually started a conversation with you that was never meant to end. Everything he does is eternal; when God starts something, he never intends for it to end hence of the increase of his government and peace there will be no end. The fruit of communion with the Jesus produces thanksgiving. We are instructed in the Psalms to enter into his presence with thanksgiving. This is the will of God for you.

Paul makes a bold declaration about what the will of God is for the Thessalonians. That word is just as much for us today as it was for the Thessalonians when Paul wrote it to them over 2,000 years ago. The will of God is not on the outside; it's on the inside. Paul goes on to say quench not the Spirit and despise not prophesyings. He tells them not to quench the Holy Spirit because he just told them an atmosphere that is conducive to him coming and staying. He goes on to say despise not prophesyings because when the Holy Spirit comes you will prophesy. This truth is seen in both the Old and New Testament. The reason is because nothing in the Kingdom happens without declaration. When the Holy Spirit comes and speaks we are to come into agreement with him and declare what he is saying, this puts the plans of God into motion on planet earth. The will of God is inward; the plans of God are outward. God can do it without us, but he has chosen in his divine wisdom to do it with us. Paul continues with, prove all things; hold fast that which is good. Prophecy is to be tested and we are to hold fast to that which is good. It's necessary to test prophecy or teaching by doing good because doing the right thing means God's will actually gives us discernment according to Jesus in John 7:15-17. Evil is to be overcome by good, not merely good will but in the action of good evil is overcome. Complacency doesn't overcome evil; simply praying doesn't over come evil. Prayer empowered action is what over comes evil. We must respond to prophecy with the proper corresponding action or the word may not be manifested. (More on the last subject will be in another lesson.)

The way we live is essential when it comes to hosting the presence of the Lord. Jesus is our perfect example; he never quenched or grieved the Holy Spirit. Jesus treated the Holy Spirit how he deserved to be treated and honored. I must tell you Jesus is my hero! Anyway, Paul the Apostle mapped out how to create a sustainable atmosphere for the Holy Spirit. Joy is used to empower prayer and communication; we are supposed to overflow with thanksgiving. The Holy Spirit is attracted to thanksgiving. When he comes don't quench him, declare what he is saying and live properly. This is the will of God in Christ Jesus concerning you.

3 Lessons to Never Forget

1. It's the joy of the Lord that strengthens us to stay in fellowship with God.

2. Prayer is a two-way conversation. God knows everything perhaps he should do more of the talking.

3. Nothing in the Kingdom happens without declaration. The words you speak create an atmosphere or infect it so use them wisely.

Notes

_____

_____

_____

_____

_____

_____

_____

_____

_____

_____

_____

_____

Activating the Miraculous

(Adam LiVecchi)

"And the third day there was a marriage in Cana of Galilee; and the mother of Jesus was there: And both Jesus was called, and his disciples, to the marriage. And when they wanted wine, the mother of Jesus saith unto him, They have no wine. Jesus saith unto her, Woman, what have I to do with thee? mine hour is not yet come. His mother saith unto the servants, Whatsoever he saith unto you, do it. And there were set there six waterpots of stone, after the manner of the purifying of the Jews, containing two or three firkins apiece. Jesus saith unto them, Fill the waterpots with water. And they filled them up to the brim. And he saith unto them, Draw out now, and bear unto the governor of the feast. And they bare it. When the ruler of the feast had tasted the water that was made wine, and knew not whence it was: (but the servants which drew the water knew) the governor of the feast called the bridegroom, And saith unto him, Every man at the beginning doth set forth good wine; and when men have well drunk, then that which is worse: but thou hast kept the good wine until now. This beginning of miracles did Jesus in Cana of Galilee, and manifested forth his glory; and his disciples believed on him. Here Jesus and his disciples are invited to a wedding. There is a very strong possibility that this is not a rich man's wedding, generally rich people don't run out of wine. Anyway, there is a lot of treasure in this short portion of scripture." (John 2:1-11)

Jesus' mother Mary comes to him with the problem knowing he can do something about it. Her advice to the servants was, "whatever he says do it." That right there is the key to activating the miraculous. It is the obedience of faith that activates the miraculous. It's very fascinating how this miracle takes place. The Jews washed their hands in or from water pots before they would eat. So Jesus tells the servants to fill the water pots to the top and bring a cup to the governor of the feast. So they did as Jesus commanded and the miracle happened somewhere from the time they poured water into the cup to the time they handed the cup to the governor of the feast. The servants moved in faith and Jesus was glorified. Our faith is for his glory.

Here Jesus was announcing to the governor of the feast there is another government at the wedding. The man who didn't have enough wine was covered by the grace of God and the miracle was a sign to the Jews. Jesus was telling the Jews that they couldn't be cleansed by water but by blood or wine. The miracle was that water was turned to wine, the sign was to the Jews was they must be cleansed by blood. It's only through blood that one can be cleansed, and it's the blood of Jesus alone who can cleanse them. I am not sure who really understood the sign. The sign outlasts the miracle. When all the wine was done and the wedding was over the sign or truth illustrated in this miracle still points to Jesus Christ.

Here Jesus manifested his glory and his disciples believed on him. An authentic gospel will produce real disciples. Paul the Apostle said something that really applies to this truth that Jesus demonstrated at the Wedding of Cana of Galilee.

"And my speech and my preaching was not with enticing words of man's wisdom, but in demonstration of the Spirit and of power: That your faith should not stand in the wisdom of men, but in the power of God." (1 Corinthians 2:4-5)

I want to purpose to you that Paul gets this truth from the Gospel of Jesus. If you are looking for a great commentary on the gospels just read the epistles. Remember the Bible interprets the Bible. Faith should stand in the power of God not in someone's ability to communicate. The gospel must be demonstrated. This happens as the miraculous is activated through the obedience of faith. Signs and wonders should follow us because we follow Jesus. Signs live longer than the miracle. When all the wine was gone from the wedding, the sign was still pointing the disciples to Jesus. Their faith was rooted in his power. Faith that will stand up must be rooted in the power of God.

3 Lessons to Never Forget

1. Jesus can use anyone!

2. The miraculous is activated by the obedience of faith. Faith in Action is what gives God glory and establishes true believers in an authentic gospel.

3. The Bible interprets the Bible.

Notes

_____

_____

_____

_____

_____

_____

_____

_____

_____

_____

_____

Overcoming Spiritual Manipulation

(Adam LiVecchi)

Often when people have a religious ungodly ambition, there will be spiritual manipulation. When people grow up in a culture of shame and guilt often they will manipulate people and not even know they are doing it. There is a difference between motivation and manipulation. Manipulation usually has a selfish motive behind it. This happens in families, in churches in the work place and sometimes even in our thought processes. If we haven't been freed from guilt and shame, the enemy will use those things to manipulate us to do things that God has never called us to do. Most people's feelings are manipulated by satan everyday of their life and they don't even know it. The gift of discerning of spirits helps us discern this kind of demonic activity that is usually played out in the soul and flesh realm. Spiritually speaking the only time we can bear fruit is when we are obedient to God. Results never spell success in the Kingdom of God. In the Kingdom success comes only through obedience to God.

"And, behold, there came a man of God out of Judah by the word of the LORD unto Beth–el: and Jeroboam stood by the altar to burn incense. And he cried against the altar in the word of the LORD, and said, O altar, altar, thus saith the LORD; Behold, a child shall be born unto the house of David, Josiah by name; and upon thee shall he offer the priests of the high places that burn incense upon thee, and men's bones shall be burnt upon thee. And he gave a sign the same day, saying, This is the sign which the LORD hath spoken; Behold, the altar shall be rent, and the ashes that are upon it shall be poured out. And it came to pass, when king Jeroboam heard the saying of the man of God, which had cried against the altar in Beth–el, that he put forth his hand from the altar, saying, Lay hold on him. And his hand, which he put forth against him, dried up, so that he could not pull it in again to him. The altar also was rent, and the ashes poured out from the altar, according to the sign which the man of God had given

by the word of the LORD. And the king answered and said unto the man of God, Intreat now the face of the LORD thy God, and pray for me, that my hand may be restored me again. And the man of God besought the LORD, and the king's hand was restored him again, and became as it was before. And the king said unto the man of God, Come home with me, and refresh thyself, and I will give thee a reward. And the man of God said unto the king, If thou wilt give me half thine house, I will not go in with thee, neither will I eat bread nor drink water in this place: For so was it charged me by the word of the LORD, saying, Eat no bread, nor drink water, nor turn again by the same way that thou camest. So he went another way, and returned not by the way that he came to Beth-el. Now there dwelt an old prophet in Beth-el; and his sons came and told him all the works that the man of God had done that day in Beth-el: the words which he had spoken unto the king, them they told also to their father. And their father said unto them, What way went he? For his sons had seen what way the man of God went, which came from Judah. And he said unto his sons, Saddle me the ass. So they saddled him the ass: and he rode thereon, And went after the man of God, and found him sitting under an oak: and he said unto him, Art thou the man of God that camest from Judah? And he said, I am. Then he said unto him, Come home with me, and eat bread. And he said, I may not return with thee, nor go in with thee: neither will I eat bread nor drink water with thee In this place: For it was said to me by the word of the LORD, Thou shalt eat no bread nor drink water there, nor turn again to go by the way that thou camest. He said unto him, I am a prophet also as thou art; and an angel spake unto me by the word of the LORD, saying, Bring him back with thee into thine house, that he may eat bread and drink water. But he lied unto him. So he went back with him, and did eat bread in his house, and drank water. And it came to pass, as they sat at the table, that the word of the LORD came unto the prophet that brought him back: And he cried unto the man of God that came from Judah, saying, Thus saith the LORD, Forasmuch as thou hast disobeyed the mouth of the LORD, and hast not kept the commandment which the LORD thy God commanded thee, But camest back, and hast eaten bread and drunk water in the place, of the which the LORD did say to thee, Eat no bread, and drink no water; thy carcase shall not come unto the sepulchre of thy fathers. And it came to pass, after he had eaten bread, and after he had drunk, that he saddled for him the ass, to wit, for the prophet whom he had brought back. And when he was gone, a lion met him by the way, and slew him: and his carcase was cast in the way, and the ass stood by it, the lion also stood by the carcase. And, behold, men passed by, and saw the carcase cast in the way, and the lion standing by the carcase: and they came and told it in the city where the old prophet dwelt. And when the prophet that brought him back from the way heard thereof, he said, It is the man of God, who was disobedient unto the word of the LORD: therefore the LORD hath delivered him unto the lion, which hath torn him, and slain him, according to the word of the LORD, which he spake unto him." (1 Kings 13:1-26)

It was necessary to read this text carefully to see what is necessary to overcome spiritual manipulation. Romans 15:4 states, *"For whatsoever things were written aforetime were written for our learning, that we through patience and comfort of the scriptures might have hope."* We need to learn from the scriptures. If we learn from the mistakes of others we are actually accelerating our growth process by not making the same mistakes.

The man of God was bold and courageous. God healed through his prayers. He was even able to deny the temptation of eating with the King. He was able to withstand the temptation of the world so to speak, but unfortunately he was not able to withstand religious pressure from someone who was his senior in ministry. He caved at the pressure of spiritual temptation. The Older Prophet's sons heard about this young man and told their father. So the Father for some reason or another wanted to meet the nameless and faceless man of God. During the interim, God told him not to eat drink or go the way he came. So the older Prophet from Bethel comes to get him and tells him the angel of the Lord told him to bring the young prophet back to his house so that he might eat bread. The angel of the Lord never said anything to him about any such thing. He lied about a spiritual encounter with the angel of the Lord to manipulate the younger man. Many people use these same tactics today— "the Lord told me" or "I had a dream" when in reality they didn't and it is up to you and I to discern what is really happening. Paul the Apostle dealt with this very same thing.

"Let no man beguile you of your reward in a voluntary humility and worshipping of angels, intruding into those things which he hath not seen, vainly puffed up by his fleshly mind."(Colossians 2:18)

So the younger man gives in to the manipulation, and it cost his life. A lion eats him as soon as he leaves the Prophet's house. Remember you live by what God has said and is saying to you, not by what he is saying to someone else about you. There is one mediator between God and man, and it's not the Virgin Mary; it's the man Christ Jesus. Look to him, listen to him and do what he says. Don't live your life through your Pastor's relationship with God. Get your own relationship with Jesus. God will hold you responsible for what he told you to do. We must not allow someone to manipulate us for his or her own agenda in Jesus' name. Often people will use spiritual experiences or knowledge as leverage to try to control others to get what they want. You have the mind of Christ and you can see right through that so be alert and don't permit yourself to be manipulated by someone else's selfish agenda or lustful desire to control others. You have eyes that see and ears that hear so pay attention and keep what Jesus has said to you as your highest priority.

3 Lessons to Never Forget

1. After a spiritual victory or breakthrough often we are open for attack because of not being alert, so stay alert especially after a spiritual victory or breakthrough.

2. We must live by what God is telling us and has told us.

3. Don't let someone use "The Angel of the Lord" or "I had a dream" or a "thus saith the Lord" to cause you to do what you know God plainly told you not to do. God will hold you accountable for what he told you to do or not do. When God told Abraham to give him Isaac he then told Abraham by the Angel of the Lord himself to stop Abraham. If God really needs to get your attention he will.

Also if you feel like God told you something you don't have to tell someone "thus saith the Lord or "God says", just say it and God will confirm his word or bring a demonstration about showing others that the word is from him. That kind of language can be manipulative and destructive to relationships, so just speak what you hear and do what God says.

Notes

Healing Spiritual Blindness

(Adam LiVecchi)

"And why beholdest thou the mote that is in thy brother's eye, but considerest not the beam that is in thine own eye? Or how wilt thou say to thy brother, Let me pull out the mote out of thine eye; and, behold, a beam is in thine own eye? Thou hypocrite, first cast out the beam out of thine own eye; and then shalt thou see clearly to cast out the mote out of thy brother's eye." Matthew 7:3-5

One day as I was reading this portion of scripture, Jesus said to me "Adam, why don't you pull the log out of your eye so you can see me." Some people don't really believe that Jesus would speak like this, but there is a sword in his mouth and sometimes he says sharp and cutting things to sober us up and clear up our spiritual vision that has become foggy. It is a normal propensity for people (who are not saved) to focus on other people's issues and not their own. We need to start living like we are really born again. What is interesting about this portion of scripture is the person with a bigger issue (the beam) is focused on the smaller issue in someone else's life (the mote or twig). Usually the people who focus on other people's shortcomings are shortsighted and can't see into the future plans God has for them, Selah. Often Christians who are searching for direction are actually in need of some eye salve so they might receive their spiritual sight back. The first thing a selfish person sees is someone else's shortcomings. Ask me how I know? Jesus calls this hypocrisy. Hypocrisy is one thing that will blind people spiritually if not dealt with. A culture of honor and accountability are supposed to be safe guards against hypocrisy. Often when there is no accountability hypocrisy grows and blinds people both individually and corporately.

"Where there is no vision, the people perish: but he that keepeth the law, happy is he."
(Proverbs 29:18)

Vision is a life or death issue. The difference between the saved and the lost is not only heaven or hell in eternity but it's also Jesus and having his mind now, which directly affects how we see the world. Approaching the scriptures with the mind of Christ will change what we get out of our Bible reading. Approaching relationships and the trials of life with the mind of Christ will completely change how we see, speak and live. Spiritual sight is simply about having the mind of Christ and seeing the past, present and future through his eyes. Often when people are looking toward the past through a distorted lens it causes them to not be able to see where God is leading them in the present moment and this is one of the ways the enemy tries to steal the future. Seeing Jesus and having the mind of Christ is the solution.

"And unto the angel of the church of the Laodiceans write; These things saith the Amen, the faithful and true witness, the beginning of the creation of God; I know thy works, that thou art neither cold nor hot: I would thou wert cold or hot. So then because thou art lukewarm, and neither cold nor hot, I will spue thee out of my mouth. Because thou sayest, I am rich, and increased with goods, and have need of nothing; and knowest not that thou art wretched, and miserable, and poor, and blind, and naked: I counsel thee to buy of me gold tried in the fire, that thou mayest be rich; and white raiment, that thou mayest be clothed, and that the shame of thy nakedness do not appear; and anoint thine eyes with eyesalve, that thou mayest see. As many as I love, I rebuke and chasten: be zealous therefore, and repent. Behold, I stand at the door, and knock: if any man hear my voice, and open the door, I will come in to him, and will sup with him, and he with me. To him that overcometh will I grant to sit with me in my throne, even as I also overcame, and am set down with my Father in his throne. He that hath an ear, let him hear what the Spirit saith unto the churches."
(Revelation 3:14-22)

Jesus starts off with the revelation of who is speaking. The revelation of Jesus Christ is supposed to renew our minds and open our hearts to the change that God desires for our lives. When he desires us to change it is always with our best interest at hand. Jesus is good all the time, and his goodness always has the best interest of others at the forefront of his thoughts and commandments. The lukewarmness of the Laodiceans gave Jesus indigestion so to speak. We don't want to be the cause of Jesus' indigestion, so we must repent and have renewed minds. We must live from his perspective. He clearly said to them repent or I will spit you out of my mouth. He didn't send them an apology letter; he meant what he said and said what he meant. Again, we can see the Sword in his mouth in action. Sometimes the truth hurts. However, once we know the truth it is able to set us free if we respond correctly to correction of the Lord. The spiritual blindness of this church caused them to not discern that Jesus was not in the midst of their gathering, and it also distorted their perspective of reality. Due to their material prosperity, they thought they had no needs, but in reality Jesus calls them five names in perfect love – blind, naked, miserable, wretched and poor. Ouch that hurts! It seems that their spiritual blindness did not allow them to see their true condition. The word of the Lord is to restore the mind of the Lord back to the church and that is exactly what Jesus did. Jesus said, "He that hath an ear, let him hear what the Spirit saith unto the churches." Here we see that Jesus fully trusted the Holy Spirit to bring personal application to the corporate word. The Holy Spirit is still faithfully doing his job; the question is are we listening?

3 Lessons to Never Forget

1. Hypocrisy leads to spiritual blindness. God wants our priorities to be in order first. God wants us to deal with our issues so that we can help our brother or sister with his or her issue as well. God didn't say ignore the spec or twig in your brother's eye; he simply wants us to deal with our issues first.

2. Through the revelation of Jesus Christ our mind is renewed, and then we can see ourselves, our circumstances and the world through the eyes of Jesus Christ.

3. It is the Holy Spirit who makes the corporate word personal and shows us how to respond to God. We must be sensitive and willing to be led by him to change even if change hurts.

Notes

Keeping a Clean Conscience

(Adam LiVecchi)

"God is not working on our faith; he is working on our conscience."
David Greco

1 Timothy 3:9 states, *"Holding the mystery of the faith in a pure conscience." Here we see that one of the qualifications for leadership in the Kingdom is a pure conscience. Leadership begins on the inside of a person. A pure conscience is the wineskin for faith. The mystery of the faith must be held in a pure conscience. Jesus prophetically addressed the defiled conscience of the religious system of his day."*

"Woe unto you, scribes and Pharisees, hypocrites! for ye are like unto whited sepulchres, which indeed appear beautiful outward, but are within full of dead men's bones, and of all uncleanness. Even so ye also outwardly appear righteous unto men, but within ye are full of hypocrisy and iniquity." (Matthew 23:27-28)

He addressed their inward climate, not just their outward actions. Hypocrisy means a conscience is defiled, and doesn't feel compelled to do what it speaks about. People are defiled from within, not from without. Jesus himself said it's not what goes into a man that defiles a man but what comes out of him. If evil and vile things come out of someone, it's because their conscience is defiled on the inside. Whatever is going on in the inside will be manifested on the outside.

The Holy Spirit communicates with the conscience. The soul is where the conscience lives. The mind, will and the emotions make up the soul, but the Holy Spirit ministers to all of those places in our lives. There is no place in our lives where the Holy Spirit can't minister. He can speak to the mind, will or the emotions. The conscience must be clear because the soul is the drawing board where God makes known his will and plans. When conviction is consistently resisted, the conscience is seared. A conscience is defiled by sin and is seared by resisting the conviction the

Holy Spirit brings concerning sin. Often people are asking God to do something public but in reality the real need is for him to do something private, something on the inside so to speak. We as sincere believers make mistakes; we are a work in progress and during the process we make mistakes. Let's say I am trying my very best to overcome a certain sin and I mess up. At that time I must confess my sin and if I do here is what God says will happen.

"If we confess our sins, he is faithful and just to forgive us our sins, and to cleanse us from all unrighteousness." (1 John 1:9)

It's our job to confess; it's God's job to forgive and cleanse. We must clearly understand our role in God's will. He doesn't want anyone to perish but to receive forgiveness and have righteousness imputed to us. Yet first we must confess.

In Luke 15, there is a great parable that illustrates the truth of confession, justification and repentance. The last parable is often called the parable of the prodigal son. However, the renewed mind knows the parable to be about a Good Father, not a stupid son. So the younger of the two sons gets his inheritance before the proper time, and just so happens to squander it. Often when people get what they want before the proper timing it destroys them. So the young man remembers his Father's servants even have enough food, so he begins to make his way home. We will pick up the story when he meets his Father.

"And the son said unto him, Father, I have sinned against heaven, and in thy sight, and am no more worthy to be called thy son." (Luke 15:21)

Here he confesses his sin against heaven and against his Father. The son did his part by confessing, but he still had an identity crisis and repentance was still needed. He came back to the Father's house and wanted to be a servant, but to the Father in spite of his sin's he still was a son.

"But the father said to his servants, Bring forth the best robe, and put it on him; and put a ring on his hand, and shoes on his feet: And bring hither the fatted calf, and kill it; and let us eat, and be merry: For this my son was dead, and is alive again; he was lost, and is found. And they began to be merry." (Luke 15:22-24)

In Palestine during the days of Jesus, servants didn't wear sandals, and they didn't wear rings. The Father was illustrating to his son that he was a son and not a servant. This is repentance, to change the way one thinks. The Father by revelation renews our minds to understand we are his children. When we know that we are sons, we begin to behave like sons. In this parable, there was confession and justification by faith. The son believed that if he went back to his Father's house he would be forgiven and he was. So the Father gives him a ring, which speaks of covenant. The father gives him sandals which is a picture of him receiving his authority back, and the Father gives him a robe and covers him. He wasn't just forgiven; he was restored, justified and celebrated. All this not only cleared his conscience, and renewed his mind, but it also restored his life. When the Holy Spirit speaks to our conscience, he desires that we respond so our life can be restored and Jesus can be glorified. One of the keys to keeping a clean conscience is confessing our sins. Sometimes confessing sin to a person is necessary. Often the enemy will try to keep shame on us when we are afraid to confess our sins to a person in fear of what they might think of us. The fear of man is a snare, and snares are created to hold an animal until the hunter comes to kill it. Don't give in to the fear of man. Find a trusted and more mature person of the same sex preferably to confess sins to as the Holy Spirit leads you to. Anytime something has to be hidden shame is involved, so don't be afraid to confess your faults one to another.

"Confess your faults one to another, and pray one for another, that ye may be healed. The effectual fervent prayer of a righteous man availeth much." (James 5:16)

There is healing in confession. Confession also helps to create a community of vulnerability and honesty. Often people love the truth but are not really honest, Selah. One of the great things about confessing sin is it helps to lift the guilt and the shame, but it also helps to create a community of humility, love and transparency. It helps slay the giant of competition. The lost art of confessing sin is a truth that needs to be re-discovered in the church once again.

Here are a few more symptoms of not having a clear conscience. People live in fear because they don't have a clear conscience. Often when people don't have a clear conscience, they can't make decisions under pressure. People who don't have a clear conscience will often live in confusion. They will often struggle in communicating with others especially people who are different from them. People who have a defiled conscience will avoid conflict and don't like to be challenged about their beliefs or lifestyle. When a conscience is not clear, one will have a hard time defining and discerning relationships. They will also have a hard time discerning prophetic words. If a conscience is defiled it is almost impossible to take one's thoughts captive and make them obedient to Christ Jesus.

3 Lessons to Never Forget

1. Through Christ we can have a clear conscience. 1 Peter 3:21 *"The like figure whereunto even baptism doth also now save us (not the putting away of the filth of the flesh, but the answer of a good conscience toward God,) by the resurrection of Jesus Christ."*

2. When you sin, you must confess and admit where you were wrong and why. (Be willing to confess it to the person if it is appropriate. I will give you a very obvious one that is not appropriate. Years ago before I was married to my lovely wife Sarah, I had a girlfriend. I will leave her name out of it. She was a pretty, nice and godly woman. I had a friend; I will also leave his name out of it. He went up to my girlfriend at the time and confessed his sin to her. He said, "I am having lustful thoughts about you." To say the least this was very inappropriate, and I personally believe it was demonically inspired. That is something he should have asked God to forgive him of and perhaps me if he felt the leading of the Holy Spirit to humble himself in that way. At that time the enemy was exploiting ignorance in the name of sincerity. I mentioned earlier that confessing sin is safer with someone of the same sex who is mature and trustworthy, now you may see why I mentioned that.

3. When you are sinned against you must forgive others even if they don't say they are sorry. If we don't forgive we will not be forgiven, which means we certainly won't have a clear conscience.

Notes

The Lost Truth of Sanctification

(Adam LiVecchi)

Often when people hear the word sanctification they automatically think religion or legalism, but that is not what sanctification is or what it's really about. Sanctification is not only a doctrine or a lifestyle; it is a person.

"But of him are ye in Christ Jesus, who of God is made unto us wisdom, and righteousness, and sanctification, and redemption." (1 Corinthians 1:30)

As of right now I have been born again for over seven years, and I haven't heard one message in a church I was attending or visiting on sanctification. There are times where concepts about sanctification were mentioned, but it was never the actual message. That in my opinion is scary and a bit bizarre especially considering the Holy Spirit's job is to sanctify believers wholly in spirit, soul and today. The message of the renewed mind is one that is very popular in our day, which is great. To old school believers so to speak the sanctification of the soul is similar terminology for the renewing of the mind. Sanctification is a result of a renewed mind. Since you have the mind of Christ you understand that you only exist to know God and to do his will. That is a simple understanding of sanctification. I really love my wife Sarah. What I love most about her is she is only my wife. I don't share her with others; the exclusivity of our love and commitment is what makes our marriage healthy and pleasurable. So it is with the Lord; he is a jealous God and his jealousy empowers us to be only for him. Unfortunately, there are many professing Christians who are in bed with the world! Yes you read that correctly. Now is the time to get out of bed with the world. The more sanctified our lives are the easier it is for our light to shine before men. When we live lives that are set apart or sanctified it is easy to hear God. Often there is a lot of difficulty among genuine believers to hear God because their soul realm is usually cluttered and infused with the world. It's like believers are positioned to be sons, but really or experientially they live like orphans because their life is not fully set apart for the Father like Jesus' was. Jesus is our example and in his teachings he mentioned sanctification and lived a life wholly set apart for the will of his Father. Here are few verses where you can actually hear the effects of sanctification.

• John 5:19-20 *"Then answered Jesus and said unto them, Verily, verily, I say unto you, The Son can do nothing of himself, but what he seeth the Father do: for what things soever he doeth, these also doeth the Son likewise. For the Father loveth the Son, and sheweth him all things that himself doeth: and he will show him greater works than these, that ye may marvel."*

• John 8:29 *"And he that sent me is with me: the Father hath not left me alone; for I do always those things that please him."*

• John 12:48-50 *"He that rejecteth me, and receiveth not my words, hath one that judgeth him: the word that I have spoken, the same shall judge him in the last day. For I have not spoken of myself; but the Father which sent me, he gave me a commandment, what I should say, and what I should speak. And I know that his commandment is life everlasting: whatsoever I speak therefore, even as the Father said unto me, so I speak."*

3 Lessons to Never Forget

1. Sanctification is a doctrine, lifestyle process and most importantly a person (Jesus Christ) who sanctifies by the Words that he speaks.

2. It's God's jealousy for us that separates us for him and for him alone if we partner with him in the process. The attribute of God's jealousy that is a Holy jealousy is what fuels our passion for a life set apart—a life that is full of Jesus.

3. There are no limits to what God can do with a life wholly given to him.

Notes

Deception and Seducing Spirits

(Adam LiVecchi)

As soon as you mention the word prophetic, there are people who immediately think deception. There is some validity to that thought. However, if we believe more in the devil's ability to deceive us than that of the Holy Spirit's ability to lead us into all truth, we are already deceived. If we are afraid of being deceived, we are already deceived because one of the worst kinds of deception is fear itself. Truth and faith go together and where fear is present faith is absent. Fear and deception in the negative are what faith and truth are in the positive. A life of truth is impossible without faith. All Biblical Faith finds its roots in truth. Often when the topic of deception is brought up almost immediately false doctrine is the first thought in the minds of most believers. False doctrine may be a very real form of deception, but it's not the only one. Deception comes in many forms. Seducing spirits are not just about sexual promiscuity or perversion. They also have a subtler plan. When we are ignorant of satan's devices we can easily get caught up in them.

Unto the angel of the church of Ephesus write; These things saith he that holdeth the seven stars in his right hand, who walketh in the midst of the seven golden candlesticks; I know thy works, and thy labour, and thy patience, and how thou canst not bear them which are evil: and thou hast tried them which say they are apostles, and are not, and hast found them liars: And hast borne, and hast patience, and for my name's sake hast laboured, and hast not fainted. Nevertheless I have somewhat against thee, because thou hast left thy first love. Remember therefore from whence thou art fallen, and repent, and do the first works; or else I will come unto thee quickly, and will remove thy candlestick out of his place, except thou repent. But this thou hast, that thou hatest the deeds of the Nicolaitans, which I also hate. He that hath an ear, let him hear what the Spirit saith unto the churches; To him that overcometh will I give to eat of the tree of life, which is in the midst of the paradise of God. (Revelation 2:1-7)

Here we can see a seducing spirit operating in a church that in the past experienced and unprecedented move of God through the proclamation of the gospel, see Acts 19:1-28. The seduction in this short letter to the church in Ephesus is about distraction. Here the focus of the church went from first love for Jesus and first works toward people to a "discernment ministry." They could discern true apostles from false apostles, but when their focused shifted so did their affections. They went from being a first love, first works church that experienced idols being burned to ashes in public to a "this I have against you" from Jesus. The seducing spirit came to take the focus of the people from Jesus to people. If the place of first love is left, the purpose of first works is lost. The first works first love connection is Biblically inseparable. Deception does not just believe a lie; it's also about focusing on the wrong thing. The fact was the church in Ephesus was correct in discerning false apostles. But the truth was they had left their first love and lost their first works. This kind of seduction is very subtle and very destructive; we must guard our hearts from this sort of seduction.

"Now the Spirit speaketh expressly, that in the latter times some shall depart from the faith, giving heed to seducing spirits, and doctrines of devils; Speaking lies in hypocrisy; having their conscience seared with a hot iron." (1 Timothy 4:1-2)

The goal of seducing spirits is to take people away from the faith. The Faith is not just about a doctrinal belief system; it's also about the life we live in the here and now. The Faith is lived out when we follow and obey Jesus. Some people have enough truth on their website to make others believe that they are not deceived. Truth is not only to be believed; it's to be spoken and walked in. Seducing spirits come to seduce people away from the correct belief system and a corresponding life of faith. The enemy's goal is to seduce people away from the faith so that their conscience is seared and they are no longer able to properly communicate with God. Seducing spirits come to bring confusion and deception to people.

Another form of deception is hypocrisy. Luke 6:46 says, *"And why call ye me, Lord, Lord, and do not the things which I say?"* The truth is that Jesus is Lord and there is no other, but the fact was that the person who was calling him Lord, Lord wasn't living like Jesus was Lord. Here we can see a person who has good doctrine and is still completely deceived. One of the things about seducing spirits or deception is that it causes people to not be able to see their true spiritual condition.

"But be ye doers of the word, and not hearers only, deceiving your own selves."
(James 1:22)

To believe the truth and do nothing about it is just plain deception. Where does deception finds its roots? Great question glad you asked. Obadiah 1:3a says, *"The pride of thine heart hath deceived thee,"* Pride is at the very heart of deception.

3 Lessons to Never Forget

1. Being afraid of deception means we are not trusting in the Lord's ability to lead us and is a direct insult to his wisdom.

2. Seducing spirits are about affections and not just sexual promiscuity or perversion.

3. Deception comes in many different forms and false doctrine is just one of them. True doctrine without corresponding action is deception as well.

Notes

_____

_____

_____

_____

_____

_____

_____

_____

_____

_____

_____

_____

_____

_____

In The Grasp of a Holy God

(John Natale)

"And Jacob was left alone; and there wrestled a man with him until the breaking of the day. And when he saw that he prevailed not against him, he touched the hollow of his thigh; and the hollow of Jacob's thigh was out of joint, as he wrestled with him. And he said, Let me go, for the day breaketh. And he said, I will not let thee go, except thou bless me. And he said unto him, What is thy name? And he said, Jacob. And he said, Thy name shall be called no more Jacob, but Israel: for as a prince hast thou power with God and with men, and hast prevailed. And Jacob asked him, and said, Tell me, I pray thee, thy name. And he said, Wherefore is it that thou dost ask after my name? And he blessed him there. And Jacob called the name of the place Peniel: for I have seen God face to face, and my life is preserved".(Genesis 32:24-30 NKJV)

Here is one of the greatest examples of an individual so desperate for breakthrough that he is willing to go to the uttermost extreme it. First, let's look at the beginning of why Jacob is wrestling. Everything that had happened; everything that was happening in his life, had been leading to this one critical encounter. By name and by nature Jacob has for a long time walked the road of his own choosing, the road of self will, and the road of his own strength and resources. Now that road leads past the Jabbok River, a name that means "wrestling." Jacob places his wives, servants, and company, over across the Jabbok River to the south side, and he sets himself on another part. Completely alone with his doubts and fears, Jacob was set for his encounter with God. This is his night of struggle, and Jacob would wrestle in prayer, and actually, end up in a match that he never imagined. By morning's light, Jacob would leave a changed man with a new identity, a renewed destiny, and a new outlook on life.

Secondly, we look at why Jacob is wrestling with God. What was it that so troubled Jacob? What has brought him to this spiritual crisis in his life as he sits alone at the river gorge? One obvious reason is his name and inner man. Jacob was growing weary of his own struggles of life even though he has had his special times with God. The Lord's blessings had been upon his life despite Jacob's inconsistencies. While at the river gorge, Jacob is tired, scared and searching for an answer. He has set the stage for deliverance and breakthrough and doesn't even know it.

He has his own baggage. Jacob had left home with a father who was disappointed in him and a brother who swore to take him down. His life wasn't really heading in the direction of his liking and he definitely knew change had to be around the corner sooner than later. That is present day life right now! This is where we now must realize and be real with ourselves. Where are you at today? Are you dealing with stuff that seems like it is all around you? Like Jacob, you as well are setting up a match that must be dealt with. Are you prepared to hit the mat? It is a plan that has been implemented in your life's journal. The question is; when do you plan on reading the chapter?

Lastly, let's look at the results of the match made in Heaven. Jacob began to pray that night. In his desperation, he cried out like he never cried out before! He began for the first time in his life, to wrestle in prayer. This is where movement begins. This is where the bell rings and suddenly you are in a battle that is not meant to hurt you but promote you. Jacob knew there was something different about this match. If he let go, breakthrough would be lost! Jacob faced his difficulty and answered the bell to the first round. God in His grace and mercy allows Jacob to wrestle Him. It was all in the best interest of his life and to bring him to a place of learning and applying. Even though Jacob appears to have won the match, seriously it was a thrown match. The Lord allows him to win, of course! Then we see the sudden turn of events, Jacob has his hip touched and he goes from winning to clinging!

There is a huge difference between wrestling and clinging. Wrestling is used to overpower and cause your partner to concede. However, clinging is holding onto something or to grasp in desperation. Morning light was coming, and the Angel of the Lord informed Jacob to let him go. Jacob responds and says, "I will not let you go, except You bless me." He was beyond serious in his prayer and serious in his requests. God knew the heart change that just took place in Jacob's heart. Jacob was now holding onto faith, rather than wrestling in fear. God was moved by his willingness to push the envelope and go where no man would dare go!

This lesson is all about prophetic persistence! Stuff you will deal with all your life. The lesson here is never give up! You will have to go for it! You will have to enter the ring and deal with what lies ahead of you. Question is, are you willing to wrestle even though you are dead tired until you get your breakthrough? The answer to that is YES! But it is easier said than done. Happy Wrestling!

3 Lessons to Never Forget

1. Never give up on your dreams and goals.

2. Don't be afraid to get desperate. Do whatever it takes.

3. The end results of your tests not only affect you but everyone around you. Don't forget it!

Notes

Dreams and Visions

(Adam LiVecchi)

"Dreams are when God opens up the earth; visions are when
he opens up the heavens." - Adam LiVecchi

"And it shall come to pass afterward, that I will pour out my spirit upon all flesh; and your sons and your daughters shall prophesy, your old men shall dream dreams, your young men shall see visions: And also upon the servants and upon the handmaids in those days will I pour out my spirit." (Joel 2:28-29)

The afterward is referring to Jesus being poured out from the tree resurrected from the tomb and ascending to the right hand of God the Father. Jesus was poured out so he can pour out his Spirit on all flesh. He tasted death for every man so that he could pour out his Holy Spirit on all flesh. We are still living in the fulfillment of this prophecy that began in Acts 2. Dreams, visions and prophecy are given to us to reveal Christ Jesus and his plan for planet earth. Dreams, visions and prophecy, intercession and obedient people who were willing to partner with the Lord Jesus have shaped history. The world changes when people act on the dreams, visions and prophecies they receive from the Lord. One generation's dream is another generation's vision. It is through dreams and visions that generations come into agreement with what God is doing by his Holy Spirit. The hearts of fathers are turned toward the Father by the sending of Elijah the prophet. It's a prophetic spirit that united the hearts of fathers to sons. That is what God is doing in our day and in the days ahead. A true prophetic spirit will restore generational unity through the revelation of ancient truth found in the Holy Scriptures revealed fresh by the Holy Spirit. Not necessarily new revelation but fresh revelation.

Through dreams and visions you can receive words or knowledge, words of wisdom, witty inventions, prophecy and what ever the Lord Jesus desires for you to receive. God can and will give you direction through your dreams. To make it more personal you are God's dream. You were in his mind and will. He spoke and eventually you manifested when he was good and ready. You didn't ask to be born, but he chose you to be born for such a time as this. You are predestined to be fruitful in every good work and to increase in the Knowledge of God. In God's wisdom this happens through prophetic ministry. Through Joseph's dream both Egypt and his family was saved because of a dream and an interpretation with the proper response. Remember God was speaking to Pharaoh but Pharaoh couldn't hear or understand God. That is where Joseph came in, and that is where you come in. God is still speaking to heathen today. Your job is to tell them what he is saying because you are his sheep and you do hear his voice. Also in dreams and visions, God speaks your language. God is a personal and an intimate God. You may see something in a dream such as a car and I may see the same car and it could mean two different things. Here is a brief example. If I have a dream with a black Infiniti in it God may be speaking to me about my past because I used to have one. Let's say you have a dream with a black Infiniti in it. God may be speaking to you about your future. Dream interpretation books are subjective; nothing is written in stone but the Bible. Always maintain the posture of humility especially when it comes to things like this. Pride is the fastest road to deception. So stay humble and God will lead you into all truth. Remember God resists the proud; therefore, he can't lead them. Humility is a key especially when it comes to understanding the deep things of God.

3 Lessons to Never Forget

1. Dreams, visions and prophecy are to be measured by the Scriptures.

2. Dreams, visions and prophecy are not to be despised or ignored. If you ignore something that God gives you, you are actually ignoring him.

3. Often when you receive a dream or a vision it needs to be interpreted. You should thank God for it. Write the dream, vision or prophecy down; share it with others who have wisdom and understanding of the scriptures and the prophetic ministry. During this process stay open and attentive to God's voice and he will show you what your part of his will is.

Notes

The Compassionate Prophet

(John Natale)

"Now the word of the Lord came to Jonah the son of Amittai, saying, 'Arise, go to Nineveh, that great city, and cry out against it; for their wickedness has come up before Me.' But Jonah arose to flee to Tarshish from the presence of the Lord. He went down to Joppa, and found a ship going to Tarshish; so he paid the fare, and went down into it, to go with them to Tarshish from the presence of the Lord." (Jonah 1:1-3 NKJV)

The primary purpose of this prophetic lesson is to teach you that you are called to do exactly what Jonah was called to do. One of the most critical commands that Jesus gives to us is to speak truth and tell people what they need to hear and not what they want to hear. This lesson about Jonah is to engage readers with the compassionate character of God. It will also help readers think about how their own character reflects His compassion to the point that they become carriers of this compassion in the world that God has made and wants to save. The primary theme in Jonah is that God's compassion is boundless, not limited just to us, but also available for everyone that has eyes to see and ears to hear. This is very evident from the beginning of the story and to its end. Jonah is the object of God's compassion throughout the book, but we see that the story ends with a question. The Lord says, "Should I not pity Nineveh?" Connected to this teaching is a very simple question, Do readers of the story have hearts that are like the heart of God? While Jonah was concerned about a plant that "perished," he showed no such concern for the Ninevites. The pagan sailors, their captain and the king of Nineveh all showed concern that human beings, including Jonah, should not perish. Compassion and the Prophetic line up perfectly. Without it, it is like buying a car that has no tires. You can start it, put it in gear, but you will have very little movement that carries a great amount of friction. It will just be abrasive and non-fruitful. Compassion allows you to share what Jesus feels. Not what the eyes see, but what the heart pounds for.

Some important points that are critical to understand is how God's sovereign control over events on the earth are processed and carried out. God's determination to get his message to the nations through prophetic evangelism is pivotal in soul-winning and believer breakthrough. Those that are called to be a voice to the church and the nations of unbelievers will be used in the areas of repentance from self-centeredness, idolatry, control and wickedness and all types of sin. These are just a few of the areas that we all will be tested in. Even in helping others, you are tested as well. Just ask Jonah. One must recognize that the voice that has been put inside of you is crying to see healing. As we grow in understanding regarding the heart of God, we will be cognizant that there is full assurance that God will relent when people repent.

Here are some points about Jonah that you will find interesting
• The Hebrew name for Jonah is (Yonah) meaning "dove". It is quite ironic that the dove is a gentle and loving bird and Jonah does not have any of these characteristics in the text.
• Nineveh was a three-day journey. There is a direct comparison here to Jesus and his death and resurrection.
• Jonah was known as the reluctant messenger.

Do not delay what the Lord has spoken you to do or say. Lives are dependent on it for their own forward progress. There are times when the word of the Lord comes and causes you to revert. It exposes the inner weakness that lingers inside of you. There are times you will find yourself running from yourself and from God. This is recognized by someone that is hiding from the pain of discomfort. This is clearly seen in Jonah 1:6 when Jonah is hiding from the truth that reveals his inner frustrations and emotions. Your identity in Jesus is exposed before men and the inner man is revealed during trying situations. There are times when the Lord will isolate you from others to reveal His heart and love. This example is clearly revealed when Jonah is trapped inside the belly of the whale (Jonah 1:17). There are many times that disobedience causes the Lord to alter the plan of our life but not change it. Even in our weakness and failures, Jesus still brings out the goodness in us and beautiful will in our lives.

We must come to realize that the prophetic is God's voice and not ours. Jonah took the sin of Nineveh on personally and took on a place of authority not given to him. Jonah was looking at a problem that he wanted to fix. Prophetic people are fixers. They want things changed immediately. The Lord continually is teaching Jonah grace and mercy but

Jonah liked living in the realm of self-pity and control. Even when the Lord makes a plant to shade him, he still reverts to putting all the focus on himself rather than the people he is called to help. How do we ultimately finish this race? How does God ultimately get His point across to a stubborn individual? Simple, by causing a disturbance in the comfort zone of our lives. By a simple change in the momentum or direction, Jesus can cause our mindset to take a sudden swing for the best. This was evident when Jonah no longer was in control of his life. Funny how things change when we are not the Captain of the ship!

All of these points that we have discussed are beneficial to your prophetic destiny. Remember, Jesus is not concerned about your feelings. He is concerned about you future!

3 Lessons to Never Forget

1. Without compassion, passion does not exist

2. Passion for people is not taught; it is caught

3. Compassion leads to evangelism, which leads to soul winning, which leads to signs and wonders.

Notes

_____

_____

_____

_____

_____

_____

_____

_____

_____

_____

_____

_____

_____

_____

_____

Being a Voice for Those Who Have None

(Adam LiVecchi)

"Open thy mouth for the dumb in the cause of all such as are appointed to destruction. Open thy mouth, judge righteously, and plead the cause of the poor and needy."
(Proverbs 31:8-9)

Would you say that a mom and dad who want to abort their unborn child is appointed to destruction? It's interesting how the poor and the needy and those who are appointed to destruction are together in the very same thought. We need to keep in mind that the beginning of Proverbs 31 declares that chapter to be a prophecy.

"The words of king Lemuel, the prophecy that his mother taught him." (Proverbs 31:1)

The name Lemuel actually means Solomon. The bride of Christ is a prophetic people that carries the heart of her groom. God loves justice and he hates injustice. Unfortunately, sometimes our complacency equals someone else's injustice. I am not trying to make you feel guilty. I am merely saying that we are not permitted to be silent or inactive when it comes to being a voice and doing what God commanded us to. We need to be a voice whether we are dealing with abortion, the sex-trade, the poor who are starving, or the rich who are really poor because they don't know Jesus. If I were to define truly prophetic people, I could do it in three words: Listen.Learn. Obey! It's not enough to say something about injustice or pray something about injustice; we are required to do something about injustice.

"He hath showed thee, O man, what is good; and what doth the LORD require of thee, but to do justly, and to love mercy, and to walk humbly with thy God?" (Micah 6:8)

When we really believe the prayers we pray and the words we speak, there will be corresponding actions or we are hypocrites who say one thing and do another.

"When the Kingdom comes everything changes." - Steve Stewart. When the Kingdom comes everything changes and justice is established. The fruit or righteousness is justice. If we are in right relationship with God, we will do justice and our fellow man will be a beneficiary of our relationship with God. That is what Biblical Christianity looks like; it looks and smells just like Jesus. He is our example, and he always did justice. If Jesus didn't always do justice he wouldn't have been sinless, but he was. Often we think of sin as what we say or do that is wrong, I want to stretch that concept a little. Sin is also what we don't do and don't say as well. We grieve the Holy Spirit by what we say and we quench him by what we don't. I learned that through a conversation with the Lord Jesus during a church service. There was a person who I thought continually just quenched the Holy Spirit by wanting to really be in control of the meeting so to speak. So I said to the Lord, Jesus this guy is always quenching you by wanting to be in control. Immediately the Lord said to me you are always grieving me by the things you say. Ouch, I asked the Lord to forgive me and just shut my mouth. We learn through relationship. We learn to care about what God cares about through continual communion with him. Whether it's abortion, the poor, the abused, the elderly, or the forgotten, we are to use our voice for the things that matter to Jesus.

"But whoso hath this world's good, and seeth his brother have need, and shutteth up his bowels of compassion from him, how dwelleth the love of God in him? My little children, let us not love in word, neither in tongue; but in deed and in truth." (1 John 3:17-18)

3 Lessons to Never Forget

1. God doesn't suggest justice; he requires it. Those who truly walk humbly with God do justice.

2. We don't have the right to be indifferent about what God cares about. Caring about abortion and not caring about people dying of aids is not acceptable. The same way caring about people with aids in Africa and not caring about babies who are aborted everyday is also not acceptable. We must care about what Jesus cares about whether it makes us uncomfortable or not. We have a comforter to comfort us in the midst of the uncomfortable times.

3. How we treat people who are vulnerable now will affect both where and how we spend eternity. See Matthew 25:34-46 and Luke 16:19-31.

Notes

_____

_____

_____

_____

_____

_____

_____

_____

_____

Operating in the Prophetic

Journaling

(Adam LiVecchi)

Journaling is one of the most important habits you will develop. Where your Bible is there your journal should be also. If we really value what God says, we will write it down. The key to receiving more is to be faithful with what you have. Before I ever wrote a book I had about 8-10 journals filled up with what I was doing, what God was saying and what God was doing. Pouring your heart out on paper to God is a worthwhile investment. On a more practical side if I was you I wouldn't buy a cheap journal. If I were you I would buy a nice journal that you will want to write in and save. What God says and does is priceless. Ten or fifteen dollars is a small price to pay to have what God said to you in a nice organized book that will last you. There are some people who would just buy a cheap notebook; the chances of them having their journals in 25 years are less than likely. The chances of me having my journals in 25 years are certain as long as the creek doesn't rise. I wonder if all the people who wrote the Hebrew Scriptures and the Greek New Testament knew their writing would make what we call the Holy Scriptures. When I say Holy Scriptures, I mean the inspired and infallible the Word of God. 2 Timothy 3:16 states, *"All scripture is given by inspiration of God, and is profitable for doctrine, for reproof, for correction, for instruction in righteousness."* I am not suggesting that my writing or your writing is equal to scripture that would be heretical. What I am simply stating again is that those who value what God says and does will write it down. Practically speaking journaling is part of the legacy you will leave to your children. Often when people think of inheritance all they think of is money, but in reality an inheritance is more than dollars and cents. According to the scriptures, what God reveals belongs to you and your children. Deuteronomy 29:29 states, *"The secret things belong unto the LORD our God: but those things which are revealed belong unto us and to our children for ever, that we may do all the words of this law."* If something belongs to you and your children perhaps you may want to have it on file. Ok I am going to stop trying to convince you to buy a journal.

Here are some practical things about journaling

(Here is an example)
Date - Month/Day/Year

Place - where are you when you were journaling.

Fasting - if you are fasting include that at the top of your journal entry. Include what kind of fast.

Communion - if you take communion by yourself or at your house write down what is going on in your heart before taking communion. I suggest you take communion by yourself at home if you don't already. You don't need to wait for a pastor or leader to give you a piece of bread.

What to Journal about?

• Write briefly the highlights and or the low points of your day.
• If you want to make confession about sin, writing it down may help. If you felt the Holy Spirit leading you to confess your sin to a natural person make sure it is someone you can trust.
• Whenever God does something supernatural in your life write it down.
• Write down your prayers so when God answers them you can have evidence that God is involved in your life. This in my opinion will really strengthen your faith especially when you go back and look at what God has done.
• Most believers don't really know how to pour out their soul to God. Learning to do this is of the upmost value. Here is a good example. 1 Samuel 1:15 states, "And Hannah answered and said, No, my lord, I am a woman of a sorrowful spirit: I have drunk neither wine nor strong drink, but have poured out my soul before the LORD." One of the keys to a clear conscience and a healthy soul life is to pour out your soul to God. Reading the word of God daily, confessing sin and praying in tongues are some others.
• Write down dreams, visions and prophecy. Test the Spirit and the Word to see whether they are of God.
• Write down questions you may have about the circumstances in your life.

• Write down any insight you get about current events. Another thing if you look back into your old journal entries God just may give you new insight.

As you write these things down you will need a code, so that when you go back to look at what God has said and done you can do it in an orderly and timely fashion. You can use the left hand side of the page for the abbreviations. Circle the letter abbreviations to make it easy for you to find what you are looking for. The more disciplined your journaling is the more fruitful your journaling will be over time.

(Keep in mind these are just examples to help jumpstart your journaling habits. Also they are not in any specific order of priority.)

T - for test, trial or even tribulation.
P - for divine protection.
H - for healing.
S - for when you lead someone to Jesus.
G - for when God tells you to give something that seems to be out of the ordinary. It could be money or a material thing, but is not limited to.
Pr - for when you receive something prophetic from God or a person.
V - for when you get a victory in your private life.
J - for when you do justice. Remember one of the expressions of love is justice.
$ - for when you receive a financial breakthrough or miraculous provision.

5 Step Healing Model

(Adam LiVecchi)

This 5 step-healing model has been used by John Wimber, Randy Clark, Steve Stewart and many others in the body of Christ. It is practical. It's not a rule; it's a tool. It will give you a grid to pray for the sick whether they are on the street or at the altar in church. It gives you a context to pray for an absolute stranger. If you know the person or what is wrong with the person you can skip a few steps.

1. Introduction - Hi my name is _____ , you are?
2. Diagnostic - find out what is wrong with the person. The condition may be visible, but it may not be.
3. Invite the Holy Spirit - listen to God and gently lay your hands on the person.
4. Command - the healing in Jesus name!
5. Test it out - have the person do something they couldn't do before you prayed.

Introduction - be polite and smile. God is in a good mood and you should be too. If this part doesn't go well you may never get to steps 2 to 5.

Diagnostic - be sensitive and compassionate. The condition may have been tormenting the person for quite some time. Often people who are afflicted for a long time are touchy because of the pain. Don't make assumptions just ask questions.

Invite the Holy Spirit - you may even say, "Jesus let (person receiving prayer) experience your love right now." Always ask for permission before you lay hands on someone. Always be gentle. (The Pentecostal push is a real turn off.) If it is someone of the opposite sex always put your hands in an appropriate place. When praying for someone of the opposite sex allow enough room between you and the person for other people to see that your hands are in an honorable place. All through the process listen to God. If you get an impression in your mind, ask the person about the impression you are getting. Don't tell them, "thus saith the Lord." If it is a "thus saith the Lord" you won't have to say any of that stuff. Often you may get a word of knowledge about someone's past or present or a prophetic word about his or her future. This really builds faith so remember to listen to God. If your impression is asked in question form you can say I am sorry about that and proceed to command healing. (This is a very brief example; I will share more details later on moving in the prophetic.)

Command - the Healing in Jesus name! We are not asking God to heal the sick. He commanded us to in Matthew 10:7-8. The stripes on Jesus' back show us God's will. We are speaking to the condition with the authority Jesus gave us. Now here is a free lesson I learned in Mexico. When you command healing and the pain moves, it's a demon. Instead of commanding healing you need to command the spirit of infirmity to leave the person's body. Again we are not asking the demon to leave; we are commanding him to leave in Jesus name. Don't pray a long prayer. Always keep your eyes opened. Keeping your eyes opened can allow you to see the spirit move on someone or protect you from any sudden movements from the person you're praying for. No where in the bible does is say to close your eyes when you pray.

Test it out - don't force anyone to do anything. You can tell them to test it out but if they say no, proceed in a gentle way. It's the obedience of faith that activates the miraculous. Be alert and cautious. If someone couldn't walk and now they have faith to walk be ready to jump up and down and celebrate with them or catch them. Having someone fall would really work in a negative way. Don't be afraid but be cautious. The dignity of other people is a huge deal. Randy Clark said this and I love it. "Not everyone get's healed, but everyone get's loved!" The most important part of this whole process is that we communicate the love of God to them in all that we say and do. If your hands don't heal people, your shadow never will so step out in faith and see God move in power.

Questions

1. Is healing for today or did God change his mind?

_____

_____

_____

_____

2. Biblically speaking are you called to heal the sick?

_____

_____

_____

_____

3. Do you have to accept Jesus as your savior for him to heal you?

_____

_____

_____

_____

Prayer of Impartation

Father, in Jesus name would you continually reveal to me the price that Jesus paid for people to be healed. Holy Spirit would you release the gift of healing, the gift of faith and the working of miracles. May I function in detailed words of knowledge especially when I am ministering healing. Let the prophetic be in full operation as I minister healing and deliverance. Cause me to move with the discerning of Spirits when they are ministering to the sick. Use me powerfully to advance your Kingdom through the ministry of healing. Let people be born again continually as I minster healing to the sick and the lost. I pray these things in Jesus' name.

Key Healing Scriptures to Meditate On

- Psalm 103:3 "*Who forgiveth all thine iniquities; who healeth all thy diseases;*"
- Isaiah 53:5 "*But he was wounded for our transgressions, he was bruised for our iniquities: the chastisement of our peace was upon him; and with his stripes we are healed.*"
- Mark 2:9-12 "*Whether is it easier to say to the sick of the palsy, Thy sins be forgiven thee; or to say, Arise, and take up thy bed, and walk? But that ye may know that the Son of man hath power on earth to forgive sins, (he saith to the sick of the palsy,) I say unto thee, Arise, and take up thy bed, and go thy way into thine house. And immediately he arose, took up the bed, and went forth before them all; insomuch that they were all amazed, and glorified God, saying, We never saw it on this fashion.*"
- Acts 10:38 "*How God anointed Jesus of Nazareth with the Holy Ghost and with power: who went about doing good, and healing all that were oppressed of the devil; for God was with him.*"
- 1 Thessalonians 5:23 "*And the very God of peace sanctify you wholly; and I pray God your whole spirit and soul and body be preserved blameless unto the coming of our Lord Jesus Christ.*"
- Revelation 22:1-2 "*And he showed me a pure river of water of life, clear as crystal, proceeding out of the throne of God and of the Lamb. In the midst of the street of it, and on either side of the river, was there the tree of life, which bare twelve manner of fruits, and yielded her fruit every month: and the leaves of the tree were for the healing of the nations.*"

Your Healing Testimonies

Below are some lines for you to fill with healing testimonies. Remember physical healings are actually lives rescued from the grip of the enemy.

_____

_____

_____

_____

_____

_____

_____

_____

_____

_____

_____

_____

_____

_____

Deliverance
(Also known as Casting Out Demons)

(Adam LiVecchi)

Jesus casted out demons and he commanded us to do the same, therefore we must. Jesus said it and that settles it. His word is forever settled in heaven, now it needs to be settled in our hearts and heads as well. When God's word is settled in our hearts and in our heads it will be manifested and established in our lives. You may hear someone say, "Healing and deliverance is not for today." Someone who says that may have some unbelief they need to be vaccinated of. It is not only unbelief; it is also deception. Unbelief always leads to deception. To say that Jesus Christ is the same yesterday, today and forever and not believe that he still does what he did through weak people in the Gospels and in the book of Acts today is to deny who Jesus really is. It is an insult to the blood of Jesus to say that he doesn't heal or deliver people from demons today. Unbelief is a sin against God. In my opinion, it is one of the greatest if not the greatest manifestations of wickedness in the church today.

Mark 16:17 states, *"And these signs shall follow them that believe; In my name shall they cast out devils; they shall speak with new tongues;"* Here deliverance is classified as a sign. A sign points to a greater truth. Satan was cast down from heaven to the earth. When he came to earth after the fall of man, he then fed on the dust of the earth. Man came from the dust of the earth; therefore, mankind literally became the devil's lunch. However, there was a prophecy about a seed that would bruise the serpent's head and the serpent would bruise his heel. According to Matthew Henry's Commentary, this prophecy was made manifest when Jesus' feet were nailed to the tree. Jesus' feet were bruised and the serpent's head was crushed. The cross and the resurrection manifested the victory prophesied about in the book of Genesis in the third chapter and the fifteenth verse. Jesus, who is the Word of God, casted the devil out of heaven and down to the earth. He also came to the earth casting demons out of people. The demons in people knew who Jesus was, perhaps because they knew the authority of his voice. Jesus didn't just cast out demons; he also commanded us to do that very same thing. When a demon or demons are cast out of a person, it is a sign that points to one day the devil and all his minions will be thrown off the earth forever into the lake of fire. Perhaps now you see why satan doesn't like deliverance?

Revelation 20:10 states, *"And the devil that deceived them was cast into the lake of fire and brimstone, where the beast and the false prophet are, and shall be tormented day and night for ever and ever."* Until this happens, it is our job to cast demons out of people and displace satan's authority by extending the Kingdom of God.

I will share a testimony with you from Haiti. It was the April of 2010, just several months after the nation-shaking earthquake that took over 300,000 lives. My whole family went to Haiti with me and it was an unforgettable mission trip. I was so grateful to be on a trip with my whole family. We all stayed in tents at a Pastor's house in Carrefour, Haiti. One afternoon a young man who was possessed with demons grabbed a hand full of rocks and began to swallow them. Immediately some of the Haitian men, my brother, and I jumped on him, pinned him down and began to pull the rocks out of his mouth. Truly the enemy comes to steal, kill, and destroy. By the grace of God we were able to get all of the rocks out his mouth before he could swallow any of them. There was a group of us standing around. In the group there was an unsaved man observing the demonic activity. The demons were actually speaking through the young boy, who was a professing Christian. This may challenge your theology or doctrine but it is a true story nevertheless. The unsaved man's arms were crossed, as he watched probably not knowing what to think. The demon-possessed boy slapped the unsaved man in the leg and said, "get saved today or come to hell with me." At that moment I turned to the man and pointed at him and said, "today is the day of salvation." Immediately, he dropped to his knees, repented of his sins and accepted Jesus as his Lord and Savior. Every time I think of this story I marvel at the goodness and the wisdom of God. God can literally use the devil to advance his Kingdom. I will not and am not making any new doctrine; all I am really saying is that God is really in charge.

Here is one more brief testimony. If my memory serves me correctly it was 2005. I was in a prayer meeting in a church in Nanticoke, Pennsylvania. There was a girl who was not feeling well. She was laid out on a church pew toward the left side of the sanctuary. I felt the Holy Spirit tell me to "go blow my shofar right in her face." So I did as I was instructed, as soon as I blew the shofar (or ram's horn)the girl started to manifest demons and throw up. She was delivered from demons not through the blowing of a shofar or because I am anointed, but she was delivered because of obedient faith. Real faith is obedient to what God is saying in the present moment. It is the obedience of faith that activates the miraculous and manifests the power and the authority of God. The Kingdom comes when we obey what the King is saying.

Hearing God is always essential for ministry, especially when it comes to the ministry of deliverance. The same way the Holy Spirit speaks to the soul of man so does the demonic. Casting out demons can be different almost every time because people are different and the demonic also deals with the soul realm.

Some Practical Tips When Doing Deliverance

• When casting out the devil there should be one main person leading the charge. Having people intercede is ok. Jesus didn't need intercessors and neither did the Apostles but it is not at all a bad idea to have other people praying as well.
• Remember we are not asking the demon or demons to leave; we are commanding them to leave in Jesus name.
• Remember to listen to the Holy Spirit when ministering to the demonized. He will give you instructions. If his instructions come through someone else be humble and open to receive from a brother or sister even if you are the one leading the charge.
• The Gift of discerning of Sprits will function while you are casting out demons. If the Holy Spirit tells you the name of the evil spirit use it when commanding it to go. If you don't get the name of the demon or demons just proceed to use the authority Jesus gave you in his name.
• What is interesting is that a lot of the practices of modern day deliverance ministry are nowhere to be found in the ministry of Jesus or the Apostles. You may hear people say you don't need to raise your voice when speaking to a demon or demons in a person. Yes that maybe true but the Bible doesn't say not to either. Just allow the Holy Spirit to lead you because where the Spirit of the Lord is there is freedom. He will lead you perfectly when it comes to getting people the freedom Jesus paid so much for.
• Remember deliverance is a rescued life, not just a cool testimony.
• In deliverance, you're dealing with the devil and someone's free will. Unfortunately, there will be times where people will want to hold onto the demon or the devil in them. The sober reality is that the person has a free will and God will honor it. According to Matthew 17:21, there are some demons that only come out with prayer

and fasting. In this verse I believe Jesus is talking about a lifestyle of prayer and fasting rather than a one-time prayer or fast to get rid of a demon.

• Jesus himself did not look for the root causes of how or why a demon took residence in a person, he just cast them out. I am not against identifying the root causes; it's just that Jesus never looked for them. Some root causes can be sin, sexual immorality, lust, rape, abuse, witchcraft, and voodoo. These are only a few.

(Just to make it clear, this is by no means the law on deliverance. The best way to learn how to react is by experience.)

Questions

1. Can you pray deliverance for yourself?

_____

_____

_____

_____

2. Are you afraid to cast the devil out of someone?

_____

_____

_____

_____

3. After you cast out a demon can you command it or them where to go?

_____

_____

_____

_____

Prayer of Impartation

Father, in Jesus name, would you use me to extend your Kingdom through the ministry of deliverance. Let the gift of discerning of Spirits operate as I minister to the oppressed and the possessed. Let many be set free and healed through my deliverance ministry. Lord let your Kingdom come as I pray and prophesy. Give me the love, compassion, wisdom and perseverance needed to see the oppressed go free. I ask these things in the name of Jesus Christ.

Scriptures to Meditate On

• Psalm 18:2 *"The LORD is my rock, and my fortress, and my deliverer; my God, my strength, in whom I will trust; my buckler, and the horn of my salvation, and my high tower."*
• Psalm 18:19 *"He brought me forth also into a large place; he delivered me, because he delighted in me."*
• Psalm 34: 4 *"I sought the LORD, and he heard me, and delivered me from all my fears."*
• Luke 11:20 *"But if I with the finger of God cast out devils, no doubt the kingdom of God is come upon you."*

Tips for Operating in the Prophetic Gifts
(Word of Knowledge, Word of Wisdom and Prophecy)

(Adam LiVecchi)

Prophetic evangelism is evangelism made easy. When you have information from God about someone that you never met before it changes everything. Countless times I have seen the Lord open and soften the hardest hearts through a prophetic word. Many times the result of a truly prophetic word from God are healing and salvation, which in the Greek is one word "sozo." Jesus moved in the Prophetic gifts that Paul the Apostle listed in 1 Corinthians 12. 1 Corinthians 14:31 states, *"For ye may all prophesy one by one, that all may learn, and all may be comforted."* Paul wanted everyone to learn to prophesy. Learning involves making mistakes. Control freaks are afraid of mistakes; insecure people are afraid of mistakes. People with an unhealthy fear of the Lord are afraid to do anything outside of what they know for certain will work. So many people, especially leaders, are afraid to make mistakes. If you are afraid to make mistakes as a leader you will create a sterile atmosphere. Some people are so afraid to make mistakes they don't even try. It's ok to be wrong; it's not ok to stay wrong.

In the Body of Christ the Prophetic has been abused, misused and even sold. Prophets for Profit and a lot of the prophetic movement nowadays is really a joke. For that I do apologize. Just because there is a nutri-grain prophetic movement that is nutty, fruity and flaky, doesn't mean there isn't an authentic and healthy prophetic movement that God wants to establish in his church today. Notice I said his church, not yours or mine. Remember this, what is entrusted to you doesn't belong to you it belongs to Jesus, so be careful how you handle it. The prophetic that Jesus operated in and that is seen in the New Testament was used to build and advance the Kingdom of God on earth. Here are a few examples: Acts 10, Acts 13:2, and Acts 16:9-10. The healthiest and most true application to the prophetic is for Kingdom advancement. The Kingdom advances through the proclamation of the gospel. The prophetic declares when, where and how. The Holy Spirit leads us prophetically. In that the church grows and is edified. However, edification is not just tickling the ears of people and telling them that they are the greatest thing since sliced bread. Most prophecy you will hear today in the church building is actually flattery with an agenda behind it. It's ok. God will deal with all that stuff and he is dealing with it now. The greatest way for the false or tainted to be exposed is by the pure, the real and the raw to be demonstrated in love and truth. With that being said let's define some things.

(These are my definitions. They are not in the Bible. I will explain them briefly and give you a context in which will help you understand them and operate in them as the Holy Spirit leads you.)

Word of Knowledge – divine knowledge about the past or present.
Word of Wisdom – a specific word that helps some someone get where God's taking them. Wisdom is a vehicle to destiny.
Prophecy – foretelling future events. Prophecy is an invitation to what could be, not always a foretelling of what will be.

Now that these three terms have been briefly defined let us see them in action in the Bible. From there we will learn how to receive them and give them. All of this is about relationship with Jesus and not just about entertaining conference junkies.

Word of Knowledge – John 1:41-42 states, *"He first findeth his own brother Simon, and saith unto him, We have found the Messiah, which is, being interpreted, the Christ. And he brought him to Jesus. And when Jesus beheld him, he said, Thou art Simon the son of Jona: thou shalt be called Cephas, which is by interpretation, A stone."*
• The word of knowledge was – *"Thou art Simon son of Jona."* Here Jesus knew Peter's name without being told it. On top of that Jesus knew his Father's name as well. The word of knowledge had specific detail because it is in line with how the Holy Spirit speaks "expressly or distinctly."
• The prophecy was – *"thou shall be called Cephas."* Prophecy gives identity. Jesus was telling Peter who he would become. Identity precedes assignment. Before Jesus told Peter he would make him a fisher of men, he told him he was Simon and he would be called Cephas. Jesus knew who Peter was, where he was from and who he was becoming.
Word of Wisdom – John 2:3-5 states, *"And when they wanted wine, the mother of Jesus saith unto him, They have no wine. Jesus saith unto her, Woman, what have I to do with thee? mine hour is not yet come. His mother saith unto the servants, Whatsoever he saith unto you, do it."*

• The Word of Wisdom was – *"whatsoever he saith unto you, you do it."* The Word of wisdom is also something that activates the gift of miracles. Wisdom is a vehicle that established the purposes of God.

Prophecy – John 1:51 states, *"And he saith unto him, Verily, verily, I say unto you, Hereafter ye shall see heaven open, and the angels of God ascending and descending upon the Son of man."*
• The Prophecy was – *"Hereafter ye shall see heaven open, and the angels of God ascending and descending upon the Son of man."* Here Jesus is prophesying about something that will be seen in relation to him. The prophetic and the open heaven find their purpose in Christ and his body. The prophetic is to reveal Jesus and strengthen his body and advance his Kingdom. Here Jesus prophesied what would later happen in Luke 22:43.

Example of These Three Gifts Operating Together

Let's say I am walking down the street in New York City. I see a man sitting at the bus stop reading on his iPad 2. As I walk by, I have a thought in my mind that he is having marriage problems. I stop and go over to him and engage in a friendly conversation. It begins very casual like, "How do you like your iPad2?" He replies, "Love it." I then ask him if he is having some marriage troubles? He then proceeds to ask, "Are you a psychic?" I reply, "no sir." He then asks me, "How did you know that?" I reply, "God loves you and he even likes you and cares about your life and family, and so he decided to tell me this because he wants to restore your marriage." I then very casually mention to him about an amazing book that changed my life called, "Love and Respect." He shows some interest in the book because he loves his wife and his children. I ask him if I can see his iPad 2, he asks, "for what?" I reply, "I am going to buy you that book and have it delivered to your house." He apprehensively says, "Ok thanks a lot." After I buy him the book, I ask him if I can pray for him. He replies, "Sure." I pray for him and give him the card of my Pastor friend who is a marriage counselor. I mention that this man will do marriage counseling if he would like, and it's free. He says, "Free?" I reply, "Yes buddy." He goes, "Well, I thought all Christians were crooks like those TV preachers always asking for money." I say, "No, there are lots of genuine Christians." I tell him God will restore his marriage! He smiles with a tear in his eye and says thank you. His bus comes and he gets on and goes to work.

Word of Knowledge was – when the thought came into my mind that he was having marriage troubles. Don't disregard the thoughts in your mind you have the mind of Christ. Sometimes by ignoring your thoughts you are actually telling the Christ in you to be quiet because you don't believe him.

Word of Wisdom was – when I told him about the book and mentioned to him about my Pastor friend who does free marriage counseling.

Prophecy was – when I told him that God would restore his marriage.

The word of knowledge was to get his attention. The word of wisdom was so that the prophetic word would be manifested and experienced. If that man goes and cheats on his wife with his secretary, it's not that the prophetic word was false; it's that he didn't hear and act on the wisdom that he was given. Prophecy comes in two ways. No matter what, prophecy is like the 2nd coming of Jesus. It's going to happen like it or not. Then there is prophecy that could be but requires us to walk in obedience. For example, God told Moses he was going to lead the people into the promise land but he didn't. God is not a liar and he didn't give a false prophecy. Moses hit the rock when God told him to speak to it. The people still drank because God is good. However, his disobedience caused him and his followers their destiny in the promised land. If you want to live out the prophetic word over your life listen carefully to God and obey exactly what he commands.

How to Receive from God

(Adam LiVecchi)

• Often we need to be quiet if we want to hear from God.

• The posture of humility causes us to hear from God. Humility makes us irresistible to the Father just like Jesus was.

• God speaks through the scriptures. Don't get discouraged if you are reading the Bible and feel like you are not getting a lot from it. Just keep reading; you are actually making a deposit into your spiritual account. The Holy Spirit will quicken you and will make a withdrawal so to speak when necessary.

• God speaks through dreams and visions so pay attention to your dreams and visions. Write them down, pray over them and find a mature prophetic person to help you through coming into a clear understanding of what God is speaking to you. Job 33:15-16 states, *"In a dream, in a vision of the night, when deep sleep falleth upon men, in slumberings upon the bed; Then he openeth the ears of men, and sealeth their instruction."* God seals up counsel in your heart while you sleep. So don't discredit your dreams because God does give people direction in their dreams. Often what God speaks in the night seasons he confirms in the daytime. Joseph's dream saved the world. His dream was prophetic about the famine that was to come. Again God can and will give you a word of knowledge, a word of wisdom and a prophetic word through your dreams, so pay attention.

Some Rules of Engagement

(Adam LiVecchi)

(I have learned through making mistakes and so I am sharing my experiences with you. I hope my mistakes save you from unnecessary ones. If you are smart, you will learn from my mistakes.)

• Don't say, "thus saith the Lord" or "God says." If God really said it they will know, trust me. (Saying it using those words can be borderline manipulative.)

• Don't prophesy with the wrong motives. That is between you and the Holy Spirit. Prophecy is not flattery in the name of Jesus for your personal gain.

• Don't be afraid to be wrong. If you make a mistake humble yourself and ask the person to forgive you. Your humility will impress them more than your prophetic word.

• The key to a long-lasting and effective prophetic ministry is integrity.

• Prophecy is not for sale! Don't prostitute the anointing.

• Don't use the prophetic to vent on someone publicly that you should have spoken to privately. The pulpit is not for you to vent on people.

• Ask God, is now the time for the word you gave me? The timing is huge especially in the prophetic.

• Give the word how you receive it.

• It's ok to ask questions instead of making declarative statements. (Here is a brief example. Let's say you are praying for someone and a thought flies through your mind that this person hates his or her Father. You don't say Jesus says you hate your Father. You don't add to the word and say your Father left you and that is why you hate him. Don't add to or take away from the word. Ask the person, "Do you have any hatred toward your Father?" Your question allows you to be wrong and them the opportunity to respond. If they say yes you most likely will have a successful time of ministry after that. If they say no, just humbly ask them to forgive you and continue ministering to them.

• The prophetic opens up in conversations. Jesus and the woman at the well in John 4 is a perfect example. One detailed word of knowledge led to a whole city receiving Jesus. The prophetic can open up cities and nations to the gospel. So be faithful with what God shows you and he will increase your influence.

Judging Prophecy

(Adam LiVecchi)

This is only a brief check and balance so to speak when it comes to judging prophecy. When prophecy is judged properly it creates a safe environment for learning as well as a culture of integrity and transparency. This is very much needed today.

"Let the prophets speak two or three, and let the other judge. If any thing be revealed to another that sitteth by, let the first hold his peace. For ye may all prophesy one by one, that all may learn, and all may be comforted. And the spirits of the prophets are subject to the prophets. For God is not the author of confusion, but of peace, as in all churches of the saints." (1 Corinthians 14:29-32)

Here we see the fruits of the Spirit and the Wisdom of God in motion during prophetic ministry. Patience is the key to the prophetic ministry functioning properly. Paul the Apostle is surmising that while one prophetic person is speaking that another may receive revelation, but he should wait until the other person is finished speaking hence, "God is not the author of confusion." The spirit of the Prophets is subject to the Prophets. It doesn't say the spirit of the prophets is subject to the Pastor. Often when Pastors try to control the prophetic, it fosters rebellion and dysfunction. The senior leader of the church ultimately is in charge, but Biblically speaking prophets are to hold each other accountable. Here Paul shows us that Prophecy is to be judged and prophets are to be kept accountable. There is no exception to this. All Prophets and prophetic people are to be kept accountable. If they make a mistake, the proper protocol is to humble themselves and confess their mistake. This is a good example that no one is perfect but leadership is humble and accountable. People who are not consumed with their reputation will humble themselves. These are the kinds of leaders we need in such a time like this.

Check and Balance List for Judging Prophecy

• Does the prophecy lift up Jesus, if it were to be fulfilled?

• Does it line up with what the Bible teaches clearly?

• Does it bear witness with your Spirit, concerning what God has already revealed to you?

• Does the word bear witness with those people whom you are accountable to? (If you are married does the word bear witness with your spouse?)

• You don't have to understand a word for it to be from God. Sometimes you will not fully understand it, but you will still know it's from God.

• Does the word help you to see your part in God's will? Does it allow you to understand what you must do so that God manifests what he said he would do?

• After the word is given, you will be tested by it. (This happened to Joseph in the book of Genesis.) When a word is from God it is meant to both test and bless you, yet the final outcome is to glorify him. We mature from the time a prophetic word is given to the time it is fulfilled.

• Does the word spoken create faith?

• Does the word give you hope for the future?

• If the word is a rebuke or a correction, it will still give you a hope.

• If the word is a pending judgment from God it will have a, "if you do this, God will do that." Meaning if you change God will withhold the pending judgment. The judgments of God are redemptive in nature. The judgment of God releases the knowledge of God. Here is an example: Ezekiel 12:15-16 states, *"And they shall know that I am the LORD, when I shall scatter them among the nations, and disperse them in the countries. But I will leave a few men of them from the sword, from the famine, and from the pestilence; that they may declare all their abominations among the heathen whither they come; and they shall know that I am the LORD."* The judgment of God reveals the Lord and gives hope through a promise. The wrath of God is the complete absence of mercy. The wrath of God is stored up for a day, while the judgments of God are for today so to speak. If healing is for today, and it is, then so are the judgments of God.

• There is a difference between edification and flattery. Edification is to build someone up; flattery is to puff someone up. Often personal prophecies that have flattery in or on them are given because of a selfish motive or a personal agenda. Flattery is deception, while edification is a truth full of grace that strengths and empowers.

• If someone gives you a wrong word, it doesn't mean they are a false prophet. Paul desired the Corinthians to learn to prophesy. Mistakes is a part of any learning process.

Practical Tips When You Receive a Prophetic Word

• Have someone write down the word for you while you are receiving it. Write down the date, time and place, and the person who gave you the word.

• If you can get an audio or video of the word make sure you do. Go to church or gatherings ready to receive a word from the Lord.

• Pray what Mary prayed, "Be in unto me Lord according to your word."

• Thank the Lord for the word and pray a blessing over the person who gave you the word. If the Lord leads you giving to their ministry is also a good idea. It shows the Lord Jesus that you value his voice. (This is not buying a word; it's responding graciously to the Lord and the person he used. If someone is selling prophetic words don't ever buy one that in my opinion is divination.)

• Read over, listen to or watch the word over again and ask the Lord what is your part in him manifesting his word.

• Write your prophecies out and when they come to pass write down the date and how it happened. This is priceless, its part of your history with God. This is part of the legacy you will leave with children. (If you are married have your spouse write down the word down, pray about it together, talk about it and thank God that, "he is watching over his word to perform it."

Hearing and Seeing Hindrances
and Ways to Overcome Them

(Some of these concepts come from a book entitled "Sitting at His Feet -
Developing Ears to Hear the Voice of Jesus" by Adam LiVecchi
This Book will be available on - www.weseejesusministries.com)

• When we come to God with a preconceived notion of what he will say, we will not be able to hear what he is saying.

• If we do not believe what Jesus has said, we will clearly have trouble hearing what he is saying.

• A huge part of the reason people presently have a hard time hearing God's voice today is because of the leaders of yesterday. (It is also because of false teaching that states God is no longer speaking.)

• A person, who will not hear correction, probably will not have direction in their life.

• Sometimes we come to a place in God where we can go no further in him unless we allow him to deal with the things that are hindering us from moving forward with him.

• Someone who does not have rule over his or her mind will and emotions will inherently struggle to hear God's voice.

• Un-Forgiveness will harden hearts, deafen ears and blind spiritual eyes.

• Often in prayer we speak too much and don't listen enough.

• Fear and worry will also cause spiritual ears to be deaf and spiritual eyes to be blind.

• Gossip, if we always talk about God's kids, what makes us think he is going to desire to talk to us.

• When we do not obey what God has revealed already, chances are he may not reveal more.

• Our ears will be deaf if we do not guard our hearts. Our spiritual eyes will be blind if there are not spiritual virtues in our life as mentioned in 2 Peter 1:5-9.

• Un-confessed sin causes shame. Shame causes people to run from God instead of to him.

• Un-resolved conflict creates confusion. Someone who struggles with confusion will not have clear direction for his or her life.

• Hebrews 12:15 KJV *"Looking diligently lest any man fail of the grace of God; lest any root of bitterness springing up trouble you, and thereby many be defiled;"* One root of bitterness that springs out of one person's mouth will defile those who hear it. Defiled ears will have a hard time hearing God.

• Despise not prophesying. When we despise prophecy, we are actually telling God we do not want to hear his voice.

• Offense really deafens ears and hardens hearts. Choosing to forgive before people they say they are sorry is essential if you want to move forward in the Kingdom.

• Bad theology caused the religious people in Jesus' day to not be able to hear God's voice or see what he was doing through his Son Jesus.

• A fear of being deceived. We must trust God more than our own fears or doubts.

Study Resources

Software

E-Sword – is a great free Bible program that will help you begin to understand the meaning of Hebrew and Greek words. They also make something similar for Mac users, called MacSword. These are both free resources. You can also download free commentaries, dictionaries and other helpful material. I highly recommend the John Wesley commentary.

Logos Bible Software – This is not free unless it is a gift. Perhaps this is the most extensive and Bible software program that I am aware of.

Websites

E-Sword – http://www.e-sword.net/
MacSword – http://macsword.com/

App's – for Phones and Tablets
• iPhone or Androids- Strong's Concordance.
• YouVersion Bible App
• Logos

Recommended Reading

The History of Redemption by Jonathan Edwards
Knowing God by JI Packard
The Seer by James Goll
The School of the Seers by Jonathon Welton

Notes

Notes

Notes

Notes

Bibliography

Scriptures marked NKJV are from the Thomas Nelson NKJV.

MacArthur, J. (1994). Reckless faith: When the church loses its will to discern (219). Wheaton, Ill.: Crossway Books (pg. 107 - 119).

Quotes from Bill Johnson, Randy Clark and Graham Cook were heard during their services or on their podcasts.

All definitions from the – New Oxford American Dictionary, that comes on Mac-Book's.

Contact Information

Voices in the Wilderness | School of the Prophets
www.VoicesintheWilderness.us
info@voicesinthewilderness.us

If you are interested in hosting a prophtic school use the contact above or contact John Natale and Adam LiVecchi through their contact information below.

John Natale Ministries

John Natale Ministries is used to engage people with the intimacy and passion of Christ. To win souls and have an encounter with the supernatural presence of God. Bridging Churches internationally wide. Helping and supporting Leaders fulfill their calling and destiny. They prophetically minister to the church under the direction of the Holy Spirit.

During the course of their many travels, JNM has come to recognize that the church needs an awakening. Their soul permeates with a passion for the things of God and they know the time is short and there is much work to be done. The fields are white unto harvest, but the workers are few.

They travel on the road with their entire family. Three of their five children are on their worship team. They are now able to fulfill their destiny as they travel through the doors the Holy Spirit leads. To prepare the way for this mandate. The heart-cry for JNM is for revival all across the nations.

John and Nancy were married on Sept 5th, 1987. They have been blessed with six-wonderful boys; CJ, Ryan, Chase, Noah, Luke and Jacob.

John Natale Ministries
JohnNatale.net
revivalist@optonline.net

weseejesus
MINISTRIES

Adam LiVecchi, the leader of We See Jesus Ministries, lives by faith and has a heart to bring the Word of the Lord to the Body of Christ. His ministry is an itinerant ministry based in Northern NJ. As a result of the Lord's leading he has had the opportunity to minister internationally in Honduras, China, Mexico, Philippines, India, Peru, Dominican Republic, Brazil, Nicaragua, Haiti, Canada, Uruguay, Cuba, Uganda and all across the United States. Adam has authored three books entitled "His Name is the Word of God", "The Execution of Jesus Christ" and "Go.Preach.Heal." Also he was featured in a book called "So You Want to Change the World."

We See Jesus Ministries seeks to build the Kingdom of God through equipping the local church and delivering the Gospel message with signs and wonders following. Adam has the privilege of traveling with his beautiful wife, Sarah, and his brother, Aaron, who are both anointed musicians. Adam is also the co-founder of Voices in the Wilderness School of the Prophets with John Natale of John Natale Ministries. Adam and Sarah LiVecchi look forward to building long lasting relationships that lead to sustainable change for the glory of King Jesus.

We See Jesus Ministries
31 Werneking Place
Little Ferry, NJ 07643
(973) 296-9050
WeSeeJesusMinistries.com
info@weseejesusministries.com

Here are some more books by Adam LiVecchi.
They are available online at www.WeSeeJesusMinistries.com

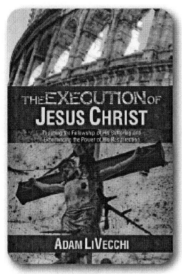

The Execution of Jesus Christ

So You Want to Change the World?

His Name is the Word of God
(Also Available in Spanish)

Go.Preach.Heal
Ministry Manual

CPSIA information can be obtained at www.ICGtesting.com
Printed in the USA
BVOW05s2025271015

424307BV00005B/13/P